ANA'S STORY

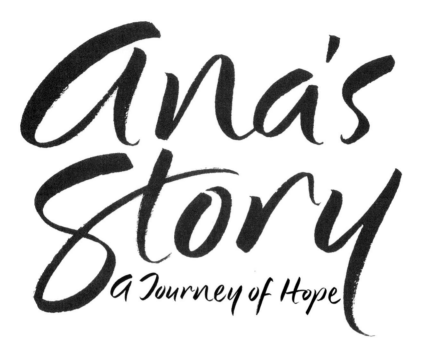

Ana's Story

A Journey of Hope

Jenna Bush

Based on her work with UNICEF

Photographs by Mia Baxter

HARPERCOLLINSPUBLISHERS

Library of Congress
Cataloging-in-Publication Data is available.
ISBN 978-0-06-137908-6 (trade bdg.)
ISBN 978-0-06-137910-9 (lib. bdg.)
ISBN 978-0-06-147792-8 (intl. ed.)

Book design by Alison Donalty and David Caplan
1 3 5 7 9 10 8 6 4 2
❖ First Edition

For Ana
and
children all over the world
who are
living with hope

ACKNOWLEDGMENTS

I am deeply grateful for my friendship with the real Ana. Ana gave her time and shared her story so that others could learn about the hardship and hope that her life represents. Thanks for teaching me so much about life and love, how to live and appreciate every moment, and how to dance the bachata. Mucho amor.

I also owe so much to all of my colleagues at UNICEF—Nils Kastberg, Jean Gough, Garren "Tio" Lumpkin, Mark Connolly, Vivian Lopez, Clara Sommarin, Bertrand Bainvel, Sunah Kim, Lisa Szarkowski, and Elizabeth Panessa Merola— who taught me about the struggles and the strengths of the children living in Latin America, who read the manuscript several times, and who made sure I represented Ana through child-friendly eyes.

The book couldn't have been written without the support of many people and organizations who offered their insights, information, and research, particularly Robert Barnett and Susan Whitson. Thanks to all of the NGOs and individuals who let me ask every possible question. I especially want to thank the extraordinary Casa Galilea program in Buenos Aires, Argentina. Also, Luz Virginia—I am grateful for your dedication and excellence in transcribing and translating hours of interviews.

Thanks so much to the remarkable crew at HarperCollins for your gentle guidance and for believing in Ana as much as I do—Jane Friedman, Susan Katz, the wonderful Kate Jackson, Winifred Conkling, Andrea Pappenheimer, Kerry Moynagh, Sandee Roston, Mary Albi, Diane Naughton, Whitney Manger, and the wise Toni Markiet.

Finally, to my family and friends who have always loved and challenged me—thanks for supporting me while I was writing Ana's Story. *Special thanks to my amazing parents, my hermana Barbara, Brooke, Gloria, Krystal, Louise, Mia, and my patient Henry for reading* Ana's Story *and giving me your honest edits and suggestions. And more importantly, for showing me that through dedication, love, and acceptance, we can all change lives.*

CONTENTS

PREFACE

In 2006 I began working as an intern with UNICEF, the United Nations Children's Fund. As part of the program, I documented the lives of children raised in poverty, particularly children who were abused, neglected, and marginalized.

UNICEF in Latin America and the Caribbean supports and advocates for children and adolescents so that they can overcome the obstacles that poverty, violence, disease, and discrimination create. As part of the program, UNICEF encourages gatherings of young people affected by AIDS. I visited a community group that included women and children living with HIV/AIDS. At the close of the meeting, Ana, a seventeen-year-old mother, stood before the group and said, "We are not dying with AIDS; we are *living* with it." She glanced down at her baby daughter balanced on her hip and concluded, "We are survivors."

I was impressed with Ana's maturity and confidence; I was intrigued by her positive outlook despite her infection. Maybe it was her vitality and beauty, or the fact that she was holding her baby, but in that moment Ana seemed so full of life.

Ana and I arranged to talk the following after-noon. We continued meeting regularly for more than six months. I listened to her tell the details of her past, and I spoke with her family members and other loved ones. The more I spoke with her, the more she inspired me. Hers is a story of survival, strength, and resilience.

This book is based on Ana's childhood and adolescence as she told it to me. It is a mosaic of her life, using words instead of shards of broken tile to create an image of her past and a framework for her future. It also embodies all of what I've learned working with UNICEF. In order to write it, I interviewed and spent time with many people other than Ana—the people most important to her as well as other children and their families living in similar circumstances, non-profit leaders and workers, and my knowledgeable UNICEF colleagues.

While I was moved by Ana's story, it became clear that she represented all the children I worked with, and I wanted the book to portray both the realities and the emotions of all the people I came to know.

This is a work of narrative nonfiction. I have written the dialogue based on what others expressed to me. Names and places have been changed to protect the privacy of those involved. I have made every attempt to convey what Ana told me of the situations and emotions in her life honestly and accurately.

Ana's story is unique, but many children around the world share similar experiences. The book is set in Latin America because that is where Ana grew up, but her hardships happen far too often to children in the United States and throughout the world. According to UNICEF's *State of the World's Children 2007* report, 2.3 million children live with HIV/AIDS worldwide, and millions more suffer from child abuse and neglect. Ana put a face on these statistics; she made these abstract numbers very real and personal.

Ana exemplifies a universal truth about secrets: Children need to be free to discuss all of life's issues—including the traumas of physical or sexual abuse, illness, or neglect—with safe and trustworthy adults who can educate them and help them handle their situations. Equipped with information and knowledge, children can then take the steps necessary to protect themselves and to break the cycle that perpetuates abuse and spreads disease from one generation to the next.

While Ana's story is compelling in its own right, the final section of this book also provides information about how you can move from knowledge to action.

It includes:

- Suggestions for how readers can help children in their own communities and around the world
- A list of websites and organizations for readers who want additional information about the themes of the book
- Myths and common misconceptions about HIV/AIDS and abuse
- Discussion questions that can be used while reading the book at school or in book groups to encourage conversations about the challenges Ana and other children face

Using these resources, you can help UNICEF and other organizations that assist children throughout the world succeed in preventing and easing the suffering of those like Ana. A portion of proceeds from this book will benefit the U.S. Fund for UNICEF.

Ana's Story

A Journey of Hope

Ana had one picture of her mother. It was not an original photograph but a color photocopy.

The image had been laminated, sealed in plastic for protection, so that it would last forever. When she was ten, Ana decorated the corners with sparkly stickers of flowers and stars. She handled the photocopy so often that the corners had started to curl and the plastic had begun to fray and come apart.

All of her life, Ana's aunts and uncles told her that she looked just like her mamá. Ana sometimes stood in front of the mirror, holding the photocopy next to her face. She wanted to see if her eyes really were the same as her mother's. Ana shifted her focus from her eyes to her mother's eyes until the images blurred and she could not tell where her mother ended and she began.

In the photocopy, Ana's mother was young; she was

only sixteen when Ana was born. She had big brown eyes and feathers of dyed blond hair. Her skin, the color of cocoa, looked fresh, smooth, and polished. Ana hoped her family was right; she hoped she looked like her beautiful mamá.

Ana's mother had been gone for so long that Ana could only recall the curves of her face by looking at the ragged photocopy. Ana taped the picture to the wall of her bedroom at pillow height so that she could stare at it before she went to sleep, comforted in knowing that if she ever forgot what her mother looked like, she could glance over and remember.

2

Ana had only one actual memory of her mother. It was not vivid but vague and somewhat confusing. She remembered this piece of her past like a black-and-white movie, the images blurred and out of focus, beyond reach.

In the memory—Ana's first—she was three years old. She stood in the hallway outside a bathroom; her mother was on the other side of the door, sobbing and wailing.

"Mamá," Ana whispered through the wooden door. "Are you okay?"

She could hear her mother crying, then trying to catch her breath.

"Mamá?"

Ana put her hand on the knob and turned it. She pulled open the door and peeked inside. Her mother leaned against the wall with one hand and turned and looked at Ana through puffy red eyes. Her mother's hand trembled as she reached up to wipe the tears that streamed down her cheeks.

"Ana," her father said from the hall, "leave Mamá alone, por favor." Ana felt confused and afraid. Her papá's eyes were also red and he, too, had been crying.

"Your sister Lucía—," he started, then stopped. He drew a deep breath and then said quickly, "Your sister has died."

Ana heard the words, but she didn't really understand. She was too young to comprehend the meaning of death and grief. All she saw was that Mamá and Papá were crying, and that made her uneasy and afraid.

"Okay," Ana whispered, backing away from the door.

She knew that her mother had gone to the hospital and given birth to her youngest sister in the summertime. She knew that Lucía was sick and that her mother had come home without the baby. Mamá went to see Lucía at the hospital every morning but always returned home alone.

Ana had never met her baby sister, and now she never would.

Lucía died when she was two months old.

3

Lucía's death was Ana's first secret. During her first days of school, Ana and her classmates marched like sailors, wearing the mandatory school uniforms of her country, white blouses and navy pants or skirts. When anyone asked, "Do you have any sisters or brothers?" she usually responded, "Yes, I have one sister, Isabel, and she looks exactly like me."

Ana considered the response truthful, if incomplete. She willingly and openly spoke about Isabel, who was not yet in school because she was two years younger, but she didn't want to talk about Lucía. Lucía's life was like a dream, disconnected and private.

4

When friends asked about her family, Ana talked about her life as if it belonged to someone else. She recited the facts like poems she memorized at school. But so many memories were missing that her past was like Swiss cheese, filled with holes.

"Mamá died when I was three," Ana told anyone who asked where her mother was. This was true, but in the place where childhood memories belong, Ana had nothing—a void. She only repeated what other family members told her about her mamá.

Ana didn't remember Mamá growing weak and pale in the months after Lucía's death. She didn't remember Mamá's face becoming gaunt and skeletal; she didn't remember her mamá's breathing becoming labored and slow, the pause between breaths growing longer and longer, until her breathing stopped. Ana's mamá was not yet twenty when she died of AIDS.

"She was sick," Ana told those who pressed for more information.

"With what?"

"I don't know," Ana replied. It was the truth because that's all she would know for many years.

5

Long ago Ana stopped asking for details about Mamá's sickness. She stopped asking about Lucía's death. She stopped asking why every morning and night her abuela, her grandmother, walked to the kitchen cabinet and pulled out an orange pill bottle and passed Ana the white pills that she swallowed with water.

Ana did what she was told. She accepted her life at face value. After Mamá died, Ana and Isabel moved in with their abuela. At age twenty-one, Papá didn't think he could raise two toddlers on his own, so he took his daughters to live with his mother. Ana and Isabel shared a bed in their grandmother's small home.

Abuela's tin-roofed house was in a poor barrio in the rolling hills just outside the city. Cars and buses sped along the dirt road in front of her house, sharing it with the dogs, chickens, and horses that roamed freely.

Ana's barrio looked nothing like the modern,

urban skyline of the city just ten miles away. Her country was one of contrasts: rich and poor, modern and traditional.

Ana's abuela worked hard to keep her grand-daughters fed. She was stern and believed in strict discipline. By the time she was in her early forties, she had already raised four children. Abuela stood no more than five feet two inches tall and had a strong, solid build. She wore her long black hair pulled back in a severe bun; only a few silver-gray strands streaked from her temples.

When Ana tried to ask her abuela about the past—why her mamá and Lucía died—her grandmother had snapped, "Don't worry about it. Just do as you're told."

So Ana stopped asking questions. She didn't know why she took medicine every day. When Ana was ten years old, her abuela decided she was old enough to learn the truth.

"Mi nieta, my granddaughter, these pills are for HIV/AIDS," she said. "You were infected with HIV when you were born. You got it from your mamá." Ana understood from her abuela's tone that the matter was serious, but she didn't understand the sig-nificance of HIV/AIDS.

"What does that mean, Abuela?" Ana asked.

"It means, take your medicine. Every day," her abuela said forcefully. "That's all you need to know."

The pills, known as antiretrovirals, help to control the HIV infection that causes AIDS. Without the pills, Ana's immune system would become weaker, and she would be vulnerable to a wide range of diseases. But all her abuela said was "Ana, this is a secret that you must never, ever tell anybody. Not even your best friend or any other amigas. Never."

Ana nodded.

At the time, Ana felt more anxious about keeping the secret than she did about having HIV. Ana didn't know anything about this infection. She assumed it was like a cold, but a cold that would last forever.

Ana wasn't worried about getting sick, but she did worry that somehow other people would be able to look at her and know. She feared that the secret must be bad—something to be ashamed of—and she didn't want anyone to find out. Ana obeyed her abuela. She tucked this secret in the back of her mind, deep into the place that stored the memories of Lucía and Mamá, the place that contained the things she didn't talk about.

6

When Ana was ten, she played a game when she took her medicine: She pretended that each tiny pill contained a delicious dessert. Each night the dessert would be different. Some nights she imagined she was dining on ice cream with chocolate sauce. Other nights she pretended it was flan with caramel, tres leches cake with strawberries, or cinnamon-sugar churros.

7

Secrets didn't matter when Ana was with her papá. During the week, he drove a taxi, but on Sundays he drove from his apartment through the slums of the city to Abuela's house to pick up Ana and Isabel for the afternoon.

"Papá, where are we going?" Ana asked, as she did every time she and Isabel climbed into the backseat of the faded blue taxi.

"On an adventure, mis hijas," he always replied.

With Papá, everything was an adventure. On their outings, they usually went shopping or to the movies or, if the girls were lucky, to McDonald's for hamburgers, French fries, and chicken strips. When the weather was good, Papá would take them to the docks, where they would stare at the tankers and smaller fishing boats moving in and out of the bay.

Papá praised his daughters.

"Te amo," he whispered to each of the girls, telling them "I love you" and making them feel invincible and safe.

While she loved shopping and going to the movies, for Ana the most magical part of the evening was when the setting sun painted the skyline a fiery gold and the street bands set up on the sidewalks. When the music started, Papá and his daughters would pause on the street corner by one of the bands and start swinging their arms and stepping in time to the music. Ana's heart beat in rhythm with the salsa and reggae drums; the energy of the music pulsed through her body. Before long, all three—Papá, Ana, and Isabel—fell under the music's spell, surrendering to the dance. These times spent dancing with her papá were among Ana's most cherished moments.

8

In Papá's world, Ana felt safe. When she was with her abuela, Ana felt vulnerable, as if she had done something wrong. Abuela never told her she loved her or kissed her good-night before bed. Ana was always careful not to say too much or to ask too many questions. She tried to be an obedient, quiet girl, as she thought her abuela wanted.

Once, when Ana and Isabel were preparing to leave the house to play with a friend, their abuela said, "Isabel, go outside. I need to talk to Ana alone."

"Why can't I hear?" Isabel asked. "Is it a secret? I want to know the secret."

"Go. Now," her abuela ordered. "Ana will be there soon."

Isabel pouted and stomped off. Ana was alone with her abuela.

"Ana, I want to remind you not to tell anyone about your illness."

"I know, I know," Ana said. She had already heard this many times.

"I'm telling you this for your safety, your well-being," Abuela continued, her eyes focusing in on Ana's. "I have heard stories about girls and boys like you who are forced to leave school because their teachers find out that they have HIV."

"*What?* Why? That's not fair!"

"Life's not fair. If you tell, you'll be treated badly. People will call you bad, ugly names. They will be afraid of you," Abuela said.

Ana was upset. Would her friends really turn on her that way if they knew she had HIV? Why? She wasn't a monster. Her friends wouldn't get HIV from sitting close to her, hugging her, or sharing her lunch. She looked and felt fine. She didn't understand any of this.

"Ana, keep your mouth shut. Don't ever tell anyone you have HIV or you will be like the others who are ridiculed and then forced to drop out of school." And that was all Abuela would say.

So Ana kept her mouth shut; she loved school and she didn't want to be kicked out. She had never told anyone she had HIV, not even Ramona, her best friend. When the bell rang at the end of school, Ana would sprint to Ramona's house, allowing her tube socks to slip down her calves as she ran, only stopping to pull them up once she got there. Sometimes Ana would stay at Ramona's house into the evening, and Ramona's abuela would invite her for a dinner of arroz con carne. Ana loved being with Ramona and her family, and she didn't want anything to ruin that.

Ana once confided in Ramona how desperately she missed her mamá. She knew that Ramona understood because she also lived with her abuela. Ramona's mamá was fourteen when Ramona was born, too young to take care of an infant. Ana thought that she could tell Ramona anything, but she never told her she had HIV. She was glad because now she knew for sure that this was something she should never tell anyone, ever.

9

Abuela didn't want to talk about HIV/AIDS—and she didn't know much about it—so when Ana was ten, Abuela took her to a children's hospital so that the nurses could teach Ana what she needed to know.

Ana was nervous at first; she didn't want to talk about HIV, even with a nurse.

"Ana, your abuela told you that you are HIV-positive, right?" asked Nurse López.

"I already know about it," Ana said. "It is a secret I should never tell."

"There's a lot more to it than that," the nurse said. She then spent the next hour explaining to Ana how the infection spreads and how to keep herself healthy. She told her the medicine would help the HIV from becoming full-blown AIDS. She also told Ana when she was older and ready to have sex that it was very important to always use condoms.

Ana's education continued at school. A few weeks later, a group of volunteers came to her fifth-grade classroom to do a presentation on HIV/AIDS. Several students made jokes. Ana was numb. She heard her classmates whispering, and she thought they were talking about her. She wanted to run away, but she didn't want to draw attention to herself. The teacher said that people with HIV/AIDS should not be treated any differently, but Ana felt different, as though there were a bright spotlight on her face, causing her to blush, illuminating her secret. What would her classmates do if they knew she had HIV? She hoped she would never find out.

10

By the time Ana was in the sixth grade, she had three secrets, and, as all secrets do, one protected another.

Ana didn't talk about her sister's death because she didn't want to reveal that her sister had most likely died of AIDS.

She didn't want to talk about her sister's AIDS because she didn't want to reveal that her mother had died of AIDS as well.

She didn't want to talk about her mother's AIDS because she didn't want to reveal that she herself had been born with HIV.

Ana kept quiet because she was told to. She didn't want to be alienated or treated differently.

11

Ana sat in the school cafeteria, chatting with her amigas about boys and the week's fiestas.

"Ricardo is so guapo," a friend whispered to Ana as a good-looking boy walked by.

"Not my type," Ana said, pushing the chicken around on her plate.

"Oh, whatever," another classmate said, changing the conversation. "Mira, look—at Angélica. She is so skinny. I bet she has AIDS. I just bet she does."

Ana froze. By now she had witnessed discrimination against people living with AIDS; she knew the only reason she had not faced it herself was because no one knew.

"Yeah, she must have HIV; otherwise she wouldn't be that skinny," said one of the girls. "Look at her bony arms. She is disgusting."

"Hey, chica, Angélica. Stay away from us with your AIDS. We don't want your disease," another girl said, throwing an empty milk carton at Angélica. Angélica stood up and left the room, her teary eyes staring blankly at the cement floor as she walked.

Ana wanted to scream, "Stop it! I'm the one; I have HIV! And so what? You won't catch it from me."

But instead of saying anything, Ana remained silent. She hated herself for it, but she was overcome with fear of being abandoned and alone if she told her friends the truth. Look how her friends treated Angélica. What would they say if they knew she was infected? No, she would say nothing. It was her secret.

12

In school, Ana covered her unease with exaggerated good spirits. When she felt down, she forced herself up, dancing through the school day, smiling and flirting with boys. She was popular and attracted attention, capturing the light in every room.

At home, Ana took her medicine every morning and night, and since she felt fine, she didn't worry about getting sick. Yet she really could not relax there, either—but for an entirely different reason.

Ana's abuela lived with her boyfriend, Ernesto. Ana thought he looked like Humpty Dumpty. After working all day as a security guard for a shipping company, Ernesto stripped down to his tight white tank undershirt, which made the gut hanging over his belt buckle look like an enormous egg. Ernesto brushed his greasy black hair straight back from his forehead. He had lifeless gray-green eyes under heavy brows. Although Ana and Isabel had lived in the same house with him since they were small, they never considered Ernesto their grandfather. He wasn't family; instead of feeling protected and safe, Ana and Isabel felt vulnerable and frightened when they were left alone in the room with him.

Many nights Ernesto and Ana's abuela drank heavily and smoked cigarette after cigarette, until the house stank like a disco, saturated with the sour smell of beer and the thick fog of smoke. The more they drank, the more they argued, creating a noise as deafening and unpleasant as a fire alarm. These evenings usually ended with doors slamming, as Ana's abuela and Ernesto retired to separate bedrooms.

On these nights, Ana played a game she called Orphan. She curled up in bed and closed her eyes, then imagined that she and Isabel lived by themselves next to a river in a house with just enough room for two small girls. An orchard surrounded the house, and rows and rows of blossoming trees offered her ripe red apples. Ana and Isabel spent the afternoons laughing and flying colorful kites into the puffy white clouds. It was peaceful and quiet.

Other times Ana dreamed she lived in a larger

house with Isabel, Lucía, and their parents. Her family, alive and healthy, would share a meal and then dance around the living room. No quarreling, no fighting, just peace. In the fantasy, Mamá brushed Ana's curls at night and then sang her to sleep.

13

Ernesto had two very different personalities. On good days, he was quiet, barely saying a word. He worked from six A.M. to six P.M., then came home and sat in front of the television, flicking through the channels, tuning in and out of soccer and baseball games, telenovelas, and game shows. Most importantly, he left Ana and Isabel alone.

But whenever he drank, Ernesto changed. He became loud and obnoxious, screaming at the television when his favorite soccer team missed a goal and yelling at Ana and Isabel to bring him another beer. The more Ernesto drank, the meaner he got. He was like an animal.

When Ana's abuela was not home, Ana usually volunteered to fetch the beer for Ernesto in order to protect Isabel. On these nights, he often reached for the beer and then grabbed Ana by the wrist, pulling her close, rubbing his fat belly against her. Ana despised his touch. Sometimes his hand slipped across her chest or between her legs when she tried to free herself and get away from him. She felt dirty and embarrassed when it happened to her; she felt enraged and powerless when she watched it happen to Isabel.

14

Over several months, these sickening encounters with Ernesto became more frequent. Ana wanted it to stop, but she wasn't sure what to do, or whom to tell. Ana was afraid if she told her abuela she would be blamed or, worse yet, not believed. Ana knew her abuela had lived with Ernesto for years, and she needed him to help pay the rent. But surely her grandmother would stand up to him and defend her granddaughters. Ana decided to try.

One morning, after Ernesto left for work, Ana's abuela was cleaning up after breakfast. She had on the same faded light blue slip she wore every morning. Ana felt the time was right to tell her.

She gathered her courage and said all in one breath, "Abuela, sometimes when you're not here, Ernesto touches me." She paused, and then quickly added,

"He does it to Isabel, too."

Ana's abuela stopped sweeping and turned to face her granddaughter.

"Ana, don't lie." She glared at her. "That isn't true, so shut your mouth."

Abuela shooed Ana away by spanking her, hard, on the back of her thighs with the broom handle, then turned abruptly back to her work.

15

Ana left the kitchen feeling angry and humiliated. How could her abuela not believe her? Why would Ana lie to her? How could she choose Ernesto over her granddaughters, her family?

Ana went into her bedroom and closed the door. Isabel was the only person in the house she could trust; she couldn't even depend on her own grandmother.

The following day Ana and Isabel played at Ramona's house until their abuela called them home. Ernesto was in the living room watching television. He sat on one end of the couch; several empty beer cans were on the side table.

With their abuela in the next room, the girls thought they would be safe, so Ana sat on the far end of the couch and Isabel sat between Ana and Ernesto. But when Isabel got up to go to the bathroom, Ernesto slid his hand under Isabel and felt her behind.

Isabel froze and glared at him, then ran out. Ana quickly got up and followed her sister.

The following day, when Ana saw her papá, she decided to tell him what happened. Maybe he could make Ernesto stop.

"Papá," she said to him as they walked through the streets in the center of town, "sometimes Ernesto touches us. We know it is not right. He touched Isabel last night and upset her. I get a bad feeling when he is around."

"Ana, if he ever, ever touches you or Isabel again," said Papá, "I will kill him."

The words made Ana feel better because her father believed her. But she didn't want Papá to get hurt and she was afraid that if Papá got into a fight with Ernesto, things could be worse. Maybe Ernesto would hurt Papá; maybe Abuela would send Ana and Isabel away. Or worse, Papá would go to jail. Her precious papá was all they had left, and she couldn't bear to lose him.

16

The next time Ernesto touched Ana, she pushed away and screamed, "Leave me alone. If you don't, I will make you sorry!"

He smirked and grunted. "What are you going to do about it?"

Ana didn't know. She just wanted it to stop.

17

"Come with me—let's go to sleep," Ana said to Isabel as she reached for and held on to her sister's small hand. The girls went to their bedroom, leaving Ernesto sitting alone on the couch, staring at the television.

Both girls felt safer in their room, resting together in a double bed with pink sheets. Ana looked at the photocopy of her mother and sighed. She wished her mamá were here to help and protect her.

Early in the morning, before even the birds woke up, Ana was startled by the sound of a door slamming. She sat up and could see Isabel leaning against the door, sobbing. Her hair was tangled, her skin red and blotchy.

"What's wrong?" Ana asked. She immediately feared the worst but hoped her suspicions were wrong.

Before Isabel could speak, Ernesto forced his way into the room.

"Tell your father and you'll never see him again," he threatened them, pointing his finger at Ana.

Ana was terrified. Where was her abuela? On most mornings, Ernesto woke before dawn and left before the girls and their abuela woke up.

"Abuela!" Ana cried out.

"She's at work," Ernesto answered. "She's not going to believe you anyway, so just shut up." Then he slammed the door and was gone.

Unfortunately, Ana knew that he was right. Ana's abuela would never believe her.

18

The dawn broke to a beautiful sunny day. Hundreds of tropical birds—yellow warblers and crimson tanagers—sang in the trees outside Ana and Isabel's window. It was almost as if nothing had happened, just another morning.

But something *had* happened. "It's not your fault," Ana told Isabel, trying to comfort her. She helped Isabel shower, washing off the revolting feeling of filth that Ernesto had left. It was all she could do for her sister.

19

That night, when it was time for bed, Ana and Isabel walked past Ernesto and their abuela sitting on the couch.

"Kiss your grandfather before you go to bed," their abuela said.

He is not our abuelo. He is a dirty beast, Ana thought to herself. She felt bitter and ashamed; she blamed herself for what had happened to Isabel. Ana was the older sister; she should have been there to protect Isabel.

Instead, she and Isabel minded their grandmother and did as they were told, even though they felt anxious and repulsed when they were anywhere near Ernesto.

That night the girls locked the door to the room, checking it twice before bed. They held each other as they fell asleep.

20

Several nights later, Isabel got up early in the morning to go to the bathroom. When she came back, she forgot to lock the door again. Ana's abuela had already left for work, so Ana thought the house was empty.

Then the door to their room opened, and Ernesto came in. He stank of alcohol and cigarettes. His eyes were wild, like those of the pumas that lived in the jungles.

Ernesto's grimy hand covered Ana's mouth so she couldn't scream. Isabel ran out of the room and locked herself in the bathroom. Then Ernesto started touching Ana all over.

She felt she was watching it happen to someone else.

When it was over, he gave Ana the same warning he had before: "Don't say anything."

Then he walked out and slammed the door. Once again the room was dark.

21

Now Ana had another secret.

Ernesto molested Ana and Isabel once, but they relived it daily, and Ana feared that she couldn't stop him if he tried to do it again.

Ana wanted to talk to someone who would listen and believe her. More than ever, she wished Mamá were alive to help her. She desperately needed to protect Isabel.

22

In September of Ana's sixth-grade year, Papá became sick and Ernesto moved another bed into Ana's room for him. Papá was so weak that he could no longer drive the taxi. Like a young boy, he returned to his mother so that she could help take care of him.

September, a month of heavy rainfall, brought sheets of rain to sing Papá to a peaceful sleep. He was asleep when Ana and Isabel went to school; he was asleep when they came home. After school each day, Ana sat in her room and watched her father. She found comfort in listening to him breathe; his presence made her feel safer.

Papá was smaller now; his body had been reduced to sharp bones—angular elbows, knees, and fingers—and his eyes had sunk down into their sockets. He looked nothing like the papá who sometimes stopped by the house in the evenings to help Ana with her math homework. When the homework was complete, the papá she remembered used to turn on the radio and dance around the kitchen.

"Watch me, niñas," Ana remembered him saying as he floated across the floor. The girls watched and followed, their feet moving to the beat of the bongo drums.

"Get well, Papá," Ana whispered to him. "I want to dance with you again."

23

Papá had good days—and bad. On bad days, he cried out in feverish rants. At first, Ana tried to understand the gibberish, wondering if he was speaking in tongues and trying to tell her something important. Over time, she realized that the words were nonsense; they had no meaning.

When she watched her father sleep, Ana sometimes closed her eyes and imagined that she was living in the past, when Papá was still healthy. She thought a lot about Navidad almost a year before.

She remembered that Papá had come to Abuela's house early in the morning on December 24, his arms wrapped tightly around a mountain of colorful gifts.

As Papá watched with pleasure, she and Isabel tore open their presents: roller skates and matching plaid dresses. Ana remembered with longing how she had sat next to Papá at the table as the whole family held hands and shared a prayer and a feast of ham and bread, mangos, apples, sweets, and chocolate. Ana's daydream ended with her memory of Papá setting off fireworks that looked like millions of fireflies lighting the dark sky.

On good days, Papá was able to have conversations. One day he asked her: "Is everything okay? Are you and Isabel safe?"

Ana understood what he was asking, but she couldn't bear to add to his suffering.

"We're fine," she said, her lips pulled into a tight smile.

Ana didn't want to lie, especially to Papá. She just wanted to deny the truth.

24

Once Papá moved into the house, Ernesto left Ana and Isabel alone. It could have been shame, or Papá's presence, or his illness, but Ernesto lost interest in the girls.

Ernesto looked the same—his legs still reminded Ana of hot dogs and his stomach still shook when he walked—but his eyes were different. Instead of being filled with animal rage and lust, they looked tired and defeated. Ernesto almost never looked at Ana or Isabel, and when he did it was with boredom and indifference. It was a blessing.

25

Until the end, Ana never realized that her father was dying. Of course, she saw that he wouldn't eat and couldn't get out of bed, that he lost control of his bowels and needed to be taken care of like a child, but she always thought that he would get better. And his constant sleepiness was not like their papá.

Let him sleep, Ana and Isabel thought to themselves. *He must be tired*. But the fatigue never passed, and Papá never regained his strength.

One day in mid-October, Ana, Isabel, and all of their aunts and uncles sat by Papá's bedside. No one spoke. Papá's breathing became heavy and labored.

Papá turned his head and said his final words to Ana: "Take care of your hermana."

Take care of your sister. Ana's chest felt so tight that she couldn't breathe. She had not been able to protect Isabel from Ernesto. She had already failed to honor her father's dying wish.

Papá died with his eyes open, staring blankly at the ceiling. Ana's uncle brushed his hand gently over his brother's eyes, closing them forever.

26

Ana and Isabel hugged Papá's sharp, bony frame. They kissed his sunken cheeks, but neither could speak.

"We need to take the body," Abuela said to Ana's uncle as she covered Papá in a white sheet.

"Where?" asked Ana. "Where are you taking him?"

"To be cremated."

"No!" Ana cried.

"Ashes to ashes, dust to dust," Ana's abuela said. That seemed cold to Ana and Isabel. Many years later, Ana understood that her abuela was not a heartless woman—she just needed to protect herself from her own despair as she said good-bye to her son. But in that moment, her grandmother's words felt cruel and callous.

Ana and Isabel left the bedroom as their uncle put Papá's body over his shoulder and carried him out of the house. Then Ernesto removed Papá's bed and his belongings.

The room looked empty now; the house felt empty. Dust and lint covered the floor where the bed had been. Ana refused to move the furniture back into the center of the room or to sweep up the dusty shadow. She wanted to leave space in the room in case Papá came back.

27

After Papá died, Ana wanted to run away. She wanted to sprint through the dusty streets, through the hills covered in tiger lilies, far away from the reality of what had happened. Ana's favorite aunt, Aída, saw the restlessness in her niece's eyes and asked her to go to the store with her. As they walked, Ana dried her tears.

"I'm confused about something, but I'm afraid to ask Abuela," Ana said to Aunt Aída. "Did Papá have AIDS?"

"He did," Aída said, looking at the ground as they walked. "He got it from your mamá."

"How did *she* get it?"

Aunt Aída sighed, unsure of how to answer. Then she told Ana the truth.

"Ana, this is difficult," she began. "Both your mamá and her sister were raped by their stepfather when they were young girls. Their stepfather had AIDS and he made them both sick."

"And they both died," Ana said softly.

"They did."

Aída put her arm around Ana's shoulder, and they walked together in silence. Ana understood the disgust her mamá must have felt when her stepfather touched her. She also understood that she, too, had this ruthless disease. What would happen to her? It was way too much to think about, so she focused on walking, one step at a time.

28

Weeks before, Ana's abuela had purchased a small crypt in the cemetery next to where her own mamá— Papá's grandmother—was buried. Even in death, Papá was separated from Mamá and Lucía, who were buried on the other side of town.

At Papá's funeral, Ana wore a long black skirt and a black shirt. She pulled her hair back into a tight bun. When they arrived at the cemetery, Ana and Isabel linked arms and walked together to a courtyard where the service was held.

Ana sat between Isabel and her abuela in the front row. When she turned around, she saw Ramona and her grandmother; she was pleased they had come to honor her father.

"'I am the resurrection and the life,'" the priest began. "'He that believeth in me, though he were

dead, yet shall he live.'"

Ana's eyes filled with tears. Now that the service had started, her father's death was permanent, irreversible. She didn't want this moment to be real; she didn't want to say her last good-bye.

"'Blessed are the dead who die in the Lord,'" said the priest. "'Even so saith the Spirit, for they rest from their labors.'"

Ana found comfort imagining that Papá had finished his labors. She liked the idea of him resting peacefully in heaven, but Ana didn't want Papá in heaven; she wanted him here with her.

One by one, family members took turns saying good-bye to her father. Overcome with tears, they told their favorite stories of his life and how much they were going to miss him.

Ana listened as her abuela told a story about her papá playing with his favorite red truck in the dusty streets in front of their house when he was a boy. Abuela finished by saying how much he had loved Ana and Isabel. She said they brought so much joy and pride into his life. This only made Ana sob harder as she squeezed Isabel's cold hand.

Then her aunt, Aída, Papá's younger sister, said, "He was the heart of every party. He danced through his life."

When the priest asked if anyone else wanted to speak, Ana stood. Her hands trembled and she felt faint, but she wanted to speak. She thought that if she spoke right now, in Papá's service, God would be more likely to listen.

She called out to God, crying: "Why did you take Papá?"

She sobbed for a moment and then continued. "He was all we had left. You have taken enough from us. Why Papá, too?"

Ana finished, her face flushed with anger, and walked away. She was angry at God; she was angry at Abuela; she was angry at everyone.

29

In the days after the funeral, Ana noticed that her abuela looked older. Her brown eyes were tired from months of restless nights taking care of her son; her face was full of tiny wrinkles that looked like the rivers on the maps Ana studied in geography class. Her abuela's once-black hair was now almost completely silver. The edge of her mouth curved downward, making her face look weary and sad.

In the early evening, Ana's abuela returned from a twelve-hour shift at the restaurant where she served food. She collapsed into a worn green chair in the living room and closed her eyes. With one hand, she reached across and rubbed her shoulder as if she was in pain. She looked tired.

Ana and Isabel sat on the floor watching a loud game show on television. Contestants in leather miniskirts completed silly dares to win a trip to Mexico; Ana and Isabel cheered loudly for their favorites.

The room was a disaster. Isabel's doll sat in the middle of the floor, and Ana's clothes were piled on the couch. On the edge of the dirty rug, one of the girls had spilled a glass of water and not bothered to clean it up.

After resting for a few minutes, Abuela opened her eyes and noticed the chaos in the room.

"Ana, what is this?" she asked. She looked around the room and sighed. "I have been working all day for you. This house is a mess. Pick it up now."

"Just a minute," Ana answered, ignoring her abuela and not taking her eyes off the television.

"No," her abuela said, harshly. "Now."

"I'm watching TV!" Ana turned toward her abuela, then rolled her eyes.

Suddenly Abuela's irritation and sadness came to a head, raising her anger from a simmer to a full boil.

Ana's grandmother snapped. She reached down and grabbed a metal clothes hanger. She came at Ana in a rage, swatting her hard on the back of her legs and her behind. Ana tried to block the blows, but she didn't cry out or beg her to stop as her grandmother hit her again and again and again.

Abuela had spanked her before—both with her open hand and with the back of brushes and brooms—but she had never hit her so hard or with so much viciousness.

When Abuela was finished, she went to her room, leaving Ana lying on the ground, her legs on fire as if a hive of bees had attacked. Isabel was huddled in a corner, watching in disbelief.

Ana cried silently. In that moment, she hated her abuela with an intensity she had never experienced before. She hated her for hitting her. She hated her for not protecting her and Isabel from Ernesto, for thinking she was a liar.

Ana looked down, examining the welts that looked like red serpents crawling up the back of her legs. This time her abuela had left a mark.

30

That night, Ana went to bed without speaking to Abuela. In the morning, she did not look her in the eye during breakfast or say good-bye before leaving for school.

After school, Ana did not want to go home. She was still angry and didn't want to confront her abuela, so she went straight to Ramona's house. After dinner, she returned home. She opened the door and breezed into the room unapologetically.

"Where have you been?" Abuela asked sternly.

"Out."

"Where?"

"Just out."

One beating became many. Ana and her abuela became two opposing forces in the house—both of them angry, hurt, and confused, both pushing and provoking the other. Ana rebelled; her abuela struck back. Neither was able to find the words to express her true feelings. Ana was trapped in a life that grew more and more painful, but her abuela was the only family member who could afford to support Ana and Isabel. Ana didn't know what else she could do.

31

During the time of Papá's illness and after his death, Ana attended a first Communion class at her church. Every Sunday, a priest and a nun met with a dozen sixth graders to prepare them to accept their first Communion. The class was offered to children over age nine, but most of the children in Ana's class were twelve or thirteen.

Ana enjoyed sitting next to her friends in the pews, singing hymns of gratitude and praise. She loved hearing the stories of struggle and redemption; she held on to the promise that her pain and poverty would someday be over and she would be welcomed into the Kingdom of Heaven.

Most of all, she found comfort there. Ever since Papá's funeral, when Ana had cried out her grief and pain to God, she had made her peace with Him. She

no longer blamed God for taking her mother, father, and sister, and for not protecting her from Ernesto. She no longer felt that God had forgotten her or lost her somewhere along the way.

She had spoken openly and truthfully and God had listened. He hadn't struck back at her or punished her. God forgave her. The world hadn't ended. The birds still flew from tree to tree, the palm trees still blew in the wind, and the warm breeze still tickled the loose hair on her neck. Ana's anger had not destroyed her.

In that moment, Ana accepted God. Even though Ana did not expect her situation to change at her abuela's house, she had faith that God would protect her during her life and connect her to her parents after death. She went to her religion classes with a happy and hopeful heart.

32

During the final Communion class, Ana stared at the chalice filled with the bitter red wine and the tray of wafers. She looked at the colorful mosaic of the Virgin Mary to the side of the altar, and she thought about her mamá. She felt close to her here.

The week before her first Communion, Ana sat in the dark confession booth and spoke to the priest about the mistakes she had made. She confessed that she had hurt her abuela by cutting her with words as sharp as glass; she confessed that sometimes she did not complete all of her schoolwork on time; she confessed that she had been angry at God, but they had reached an understanding. Ana did not tell the priest about the HIV or Ernesto; these secrets belonged to her. She didn't feel guilty about keeping them. She was not responsible for being born with HIV or for what Ernesto had done to her in the dark. Even if she wanted to tell, she couldn't forget her abuela's words: *Don't tell anyone, ever.*

On the day of her first Communion, Ana dressed in the traditional white lace dress with a veil covering her eyes. She looked at her reflection in the mirror and prayed to God and her parents, asking, "Papá, ayúdame, help me. Mamá, protégeme, protect me."

The class met about an hour before the ceremony began for their final preparation. The priest asked each of the students if they had any questions. He then told them to write a letter stating their hopes for a future with God in their lives.

Ana didn't know where to begin. When she was in church, she felt closer to her parents; she could close her eyes and feel Mamá and Papá watching over her, reminding her that everything would be okay. As soon as she opened her eyes, however, she was reminded of the void their deaths had left in her life.

Thinking of her parents and her life with her grandmother, Ana picked up the pen and began to write. She didn't think about what might happen as a result. She honestly opened her heart and wrote:

Ana's Story

I want to be in a house without abuse.
I don't want to fight anymore. I am tired of the
bruises that cover my body and the darkness in
my heart. I wish my parents were here
to protect me and my sister.
Protect me, Dios. Protect us.

When she was finished, Ana folded the page in half, handed it to the priest, and took her place in front of the congregation.

33

After the ceremony, Ana and her entire family—aunts, uncles, and cousins—returned to the house for a celebration. Ana's abuela fixed a feast of arroz con pollo, pig's feet, fried yucca, sweets, fried plantains, and fried tortillas with cheese and chorizo. Ana loved food, and she and her family rarely had this much to eat, except on holidays. Ana beamed with joy, proud of her accomplishment and excited that this banquet was for her.

"You look beautiful," said Aunt Aída, giving her a hug. "I am so proud of you." These were words Ana rarely heard. This day was very special for her, and she felt that perhaps things would be different now.

34

The following Saturday morning, a policeman knocked on the door. Abuela answered, surprised to see a uniformed officer on her porch.

"May I come in?" he asked, showing her his badge. Ana and Isabel were in their bedroom, listening.

"Of course," she said. "Is everything all right? Is Ernesto okay?"

The policeman stepped just inside the doorway.

"I understand that there has been trouble with your granddaughter Ana," he said.

"Ana?" her abuela said. "No, Ana is fine."

He then told her that he had been contacted by the priest from the church. He told her what the priest had said in his report.

As Ana listened from her bedroom, she panicked, knowing the policeman was in her house in response to the letter she wrote and fearing the beating she would receive as soon as he left.

"What are you talking about? Did Ana say this? Who said this?" her abuela asked, her voice growing louder and more impatient with every word.

"It doesn't matter who," said the policeman.

"I'm a good mother, a good grandmother," she said. "I took these children in when their mother died. I've taken care of them for ten years."

"I'm sorry. Please calm down and let's talk about this."

But like a sudden rainstorm, Abuela's mood changed. It was as though she suddenly gave up. She sighed deeply and said, "If she wants to leave, take her. Take them both."

She then turned her back and left the room. Ana was shocked. What would happen to her and Isabel now? Where would they go? She should have kept quiet, just like Abuela had said.

35

With all of their clothes and toys stuffed into one plastic garbage bag, Ana and Isabel went to their great-aunt Sonia's house a few miles away. Sonia wasn't overly eager to have them. She struggled to feed, educate, and provide the bare necessities for her own children and grandchildren, but she was the only relative willing and financially capable of taking them in at the time.

Sonia's house was much smaller than Abuela's house. The girls shared two bedrooms, a kitchen, and a small dining room with eleven other relatives. Ana and Isabel bunked with their twenty-year-old cousin, Susana, her husband, and their three children, all under the age of four, in one bedroom.

Ana and Isabel didn't have any space to play or talk privately, but they were relieved to be away from

Ernesto and the beatings. That evening Ana lay in her bed, listening to the chorus of breathing and snoring that surrounded her in the small room. Rather than feeling crowded, she felt comforted, like a puppy curling up with her littermates before drifting off to sleep.

36

A few weeks after Ana arrived at Sonia's house, she graduated from the sixth grade. She knew that no one in her family had ever been to university. She wanted to be the first in her family to complete secondary school and go to college; she felt she was well on her way.

Ana's graduation was a combination of joy and sadness. It was a significant accomplishment, and Ana was pleased to earn her diploma; but she was sad because Mamá and Papá weren't there with the other parents carrying balloons and cheering loudly for their children.

After the ceremony, her school hosted a party for the graduates and their families at the neighborhood pool. Ana swam with her friends, and later that night, when the sun dropped behind the lush green hills, she ate fried plantains and fried potatoes.

As Ana finished eating, she looked up to see that her aunt Aída had joined the celebration. She smiled and waved at her. As twilight turned to starlight and stars filled the sky like candles lit for loved ones in church, Ana and Aída kicked off their shoes and started to dance. Ana knew that Aída couldn't take her and Isabel in because she had two small children at home and a baby on the way. Aída couldn't afford to feed two more mouths, but she knew that her aunt loved her, and that was enough for now.

37

After summer, Aunt Sonia enrolled Ana in seventh grade at the local secondary school. Ana made friends easily and soon began scribbling notes and giggling with Yolanda, her new best friend. Ana loved Yolanda's easy manner and quick laugh. She felt close to her because both of them lived without a father.

After school, Ana spent as much time as she could at Yolanda's house. Yolanda's mamá knew that Ana's parents had died and that she had to move away from her abuela, so she went out of her way to welcome Ana lovingly into her home. Yolanda's papá had left them years before, so there was plenty of room at the table for Ana to join them for dinner. Yolanda's mamá often took time to braid Ana's long hair and, best of all, sometimes she called Ana "mi amor"—my love. When she was in Yolanda's home, Ana didn't feel angry or ashamed, and

she didn't feel burdened by her past.

Ana often told her aunt Sonia that she and Yolanda had homework to do or that Yolanda's mother needed help cleaning the house or pulling weeds in the yard— any excuse to spend time with them. Most days, no one cared that Ana was gone—no one except Isabel. Ana knew that Isabel felt abandoned and lonely when Ana spent time with her new friend, and did her best to make it up to her.

When they were together, Ana and Yolanda danced and gossiped, tried on makeup, and experimented with new hairstyles. When Ana ate dinner at Yolanda's house, she always excused herself after eating to take her HIV/AIDS medication in private.

On the nights Ana slept over at Yolanda's house, they whispered until the early morning hours, Ana confiding about how much she missed Mamá and Papá, how lonely she sometimes felt, and how her abuela used to hit her. Yet even on those nights when the girls opened up to each other, Ana didn't share everything. She still did not trust anyone with her deepest secrets: that she was HIV-positive and what Ernesto had done to her. Ana didn't want to reveal these truths about herself because as long as she kept them hidden, they weren't really a part of her.

38

Once a month, Ana did not visit Yolanda after school, and she did not tell her friend where she was going. On these days, Ana walked several blocks and waited on the street corner for the bus that took her from her barrio to the children's hospital in the city.

Ana loved the buses; they looked like moving fiestas. They were painted with vivid graffitilike images of the Virgin Mary and Jesus posing with Bugs Bunny and the Tasmanian Devil. Strings of red, teal, and lavender lights hung around the windows, which were always open, allowing a dusty breeze to blow through.

When the bus arrived, Ana boarded and found a seat by the window. She stared out and imagined she was traveling to visit her father in his apartment in the city. She wished more than anything that her papá was still alive.

Instead, she got off the bus when it stopped in front of the hospital. She made her way through the labyrinth of corridors, never needing to pause or ask for directions. She was used to this by now. She ended by pushing open the door marked Infectious Diseases Unit.

"Hola, Nurse López. ¿Cómo está?" Ana asked, smiling politely at the nurse sitting behind the counter.

"Hola, Ana," the nurse responded politely. "I'm fine; how are you feeling?"

"Bien, I'm feeling great," Ana said. "I'm just here for my medicine." Since she had moved in with Aunt Sonia, Ana had been picking up her medication on her own. Aunt Sonia knew Ana was HIV-positive, but she didn't have time to go into the city and pick up the medication.

"Of course," the nurse said.

The nurse counted out the white pills and put them in a small bottle. She asked Ana to sign a form and then handed the pills and a receipt to her.

Ana thanked the nurse and left. Sometimes she stayed for an AIDS-education program to learn more about staying healthy and preventing the spread of HIV. Every three months she had checkups and blood work. Ana's trips to the hospital had become as familiar as breathing, as waking up every morning and looking at the picture of her mamá.

39

Whenever Ana walked from Yolanda's home to Aunt Sonia's house, the tension increased with every step. She had begun to hate it there. No one told her that they loved her or that she was pretty or smart; no one thanked her for helping with the dishes or taking out the trash; no one hugged her or braided her hair. She wasn't valued as a member of the family. She was sure she was an unwelcome burden.

She left Yolanda's feeling like a normal thirteen-year-old girl, but by the time she arrived at Aunt Sonia's house, she was hostile and angry, ready to strike out and defend herself—which she had to do regularly. Ana had become a fighter; she didn't usually start the confrontation, but she no longer backed down when she was being bullied.

Ana's great-aunt and her cousin Susana treated her like the dirt on the roads of the barrio. If Ana walked into the house five minutes late after school, Aunt Sonia would yell at her.

"What have you been doing?" she asked. "What are you, a tramp?"

If Ana talked back, her aunt reached for a fly-swatter or an extension cord and whipped her with it.

At first the beatings were mild, but as the months passed, the punishments became harsher, more severe, and more frequent. Ana and her great-aunt developed a dialogue, a dance, both of them knowing how the other would respond. Both sides refused to back down. It had become a contest of wills. Ana's razor-sharp attitude versus Sonia's strict authority were opposing forces working against each other.

Ana wouldn't allow herself to be a victim anymore. All the anger she felt—at Ernesto for hurting her, at her abuela for not protecting her, at her mother's and father's deaths, at her great-aunt and cousins for not loving and accepting her—all of this anger simmered inside her, waiting for someone to provoke a response. Every incident at home became an outlet for both physical and emotional pain.

Ana would defend herself, her voice as sharp as a machete. "Don't touch me. Don't you dare touch me, you old witch. Don't touch Isabel or me."

Aunt Sonia would not accept Ana's new edge or the disrespect in her voice, and only punished her more.

Susana often initiated the confrontations, as if teasing and hitting Ana were entertainment when the telenovelas were boring. Once, when Ana was an hour late returning from Yolanda's house, Susana took pleasure in announcing, "Mamá, Ana is *very* late today."

Ana was forced to kneel in a corner of the house while Susana, her husband, and her children laughed at her. Isabel was the only one who didn't laugh; instead she stayed in her room. She was unable to protect Ana and unable to watch her pain. Ana stayed in the corner for two hours, her back and knees aching, while everyone else in the household sat on the couch watching television.

Ana almost welcomed the pain; she felt comfortable with it because it confirmed what she already believed about herself—that she deserved to be hurt—that something was wrong with her. No one but Isabel loved her now. Imagine what would happen if they knew the whole truth, if they knew all her secrets. Wasn't that why Abuela had told her to keep her mouth shut?

40

Ana accepted the beatings in her home, but she was deeply humiliated when her aunt or cousin hit her in public. To avoid embarrassing encounters, Ana usually remained quiet and passive when she was out with her family, but if Ana was belligerent or talked back, they openly slapped or kicked her.

Worse than the pain of the beatings was the shame she felt when she looked up and saw someone she knew from school standing across the street, witnessing the entire event. Most of the time her friends turned away when they recognized Ana, trying to spare her embarrassment, so that when they met at school the following day, they could ignore the incident. Ana was unhappy, she was hurt, and she needed help.

41

Ana's favorite teacher at school was Señor García. He spent some class time talking with his students—and listening. He talked with them about their plans for the weekend, their plans for the summer, their plans for the rest of their lives. He encouraged them to open up if they had any problems at school or at home.

Señor García was much younger and more re-laxed than most of the other teachers. He dressed in guayaberas and blue jeans instead of the more formal clothes that most of his colleagues wore, and he used pop culture and humor in his classes. He was a terrific teacher and his students loved him.

"Ana, please stay after class a moment," Señor García said one day.

After the other students filed out to their lockers, Señor García closed the door and turned to Ana.

"I don't mean to embarrass you, but I have noticed that you have bruises on your arms and legs," he said gently. "Are you okay? I want you to know that it's safe to talk to me."

"I'm fine," Ana said instinctively while pulling the sleeves of her uniform down to cover the bruises. She was ashamed that her bruises were visible to anyone who chose to notice.

"I mean, my great-aunt, she sometimes . . ." Ana paused, then continued. "She sometimes hits and kicks me." With that, the words flowed out. She told him about how her great-aunt beat and humiliated her. She told him that she had been taken from her abuela's house before that for the same reason.

"I want to leave my aunt Sonia's house," she confided, "but I don't want to leave my sister, Isabel. I don't know what to do."

"I will try to help you," Señor García said reassuringly, and Ana believed him.

42

Speaking with Señor García gave Ana the courage to try to change her situation. On her way home, she went directly to Yolanda's mamá and said, "I am not happy at my great-aunt's house. Can I live here with you for a while? ¿Por favor?"

Ana held her breath, feeling reckless for asking so much, for risking so much; if Yolanda's mamá said no, Ana would feel rejected and hurt and nothing would be the same at Yolanda's anymore.

"Of course, Ana," came the reply. Yolanda's mamá hugged Ana gently, making an effort to avoid her bruises.

Ana rushed home and gathered her clothes in a bag. Her heart stopped when she looked at the twin bed she shared with Isabel; she would have to leave her sister behind.

But Isabel didn't have the same trouble with Aunt Sonia. Isabel seemed to shrink back and become invisible when her great-aunt's temper flared. Isabel avoided confrontation, and usually she avoided the beatings as well.

"Isabel will be fine for now," Ana told herself. "I'll try to get Yolanda's mother to take her, too." This simple wish was enough to make Ana comfortable with her decision. She wouldn't disappoint her father: Ana would take care of her sister, but she'd have to wait a little and come back for her later.

Isabel wasn't home from school yet, so Ana didn't have a chance to explain the situation to her. Ana grabbed a pen and scribbled a note to Isabel on the back of her algebra homework:

Hi, hermana,
I have gone to Yolanda's house. She and her
mamá said that I could live with them for
a while. I can't stand this abuse anymore.
I promise I will come back for you.
I will protect you.
Te amo.
Tu hermana,
Ana

43

That night, Ana had trouble falling asleep. Señor García had called Yolanda's mother that evening, explaining that he would help file the papers if the family was willing to legally adopt Ana. Yolanda's mamá loved Ana like a daughter, and she said she would seriously consider the matter.

Ana knew that before she could allow Yolanda's mamá to adopt her, she had to tell her the truth about her illness. It wouldn't be fair to the family otherwise.

The next morning, Ana woke up and found Yolanda and her mother sitting at the kitchen table, eating eggs and fried plantains for breakfast. The pinks and yellows of the sunrise brightened the room. A plate of food for her sat on the small table.

Ana sat down. Before she could eat a single bite, she needed to unburden herself.

"There is something you should know," Ana started. "I have . . ." She stopped and looked down at her plate. She couldn't find the words. What if she told them the truth and they told her that she couldn't stay with them? Where would she go?

Ana took a deep breath and started again.

"I am infected with HIV," she blurted out. "I was infected by my parents. They both died, but as long as I take my medicine I'll be fine. You won't catch it from me by living in the same house. You will be okay."

Ana looked up at Yolanda's mamá. Tears flooded from Ana's eyes.

"Yes," Yolanda said, reaching out to her. "It will be okay."

Yolanda's mamá wiped the tears from Ana's eyes and said, "You can stay here. Now, eat. Your breakfast is getting cold."

Ana hadn't expected acceptance to come so easily. She hadn't expected to be treated like a normal teenager, even if she was one living with HIV.

44

For several days, Ana went to school in the morning and returned home to Yolanda's house in the afternoon. She missed Isabel and worried that her great-aunt Sonia would punish her now that Ana was gone. But Ana was afraid to call or stop by the house; she didn't want to confront Sonia. She had nothing to say to her, and she knew they would just argue, or worse.

Señor García had filed paperwork so that Ana could stay legally with Yolanda's family while the details of the adoption were worked out. Ana had to appear before a local judge so that Yolanda's mamá could receive temporary custody.

Ana's palms were sweaty when she went into the judge's chamber. His desk was covered with stacks of work. He opened a manila folder and pulled out several sheets of paper. After glancing over them, he looked up over the edge of his glasses at Ana and Yolanda and her mamá.

"You are?" he asked, nodding in Ana's direction.

"I'm Ana."

"Well, Ana, this isn't going to work," he said. "You can't be adopted by a non–family member, not without the approval of the other relatives."

Ana's heart froze. Her great-aunt and her abuela would never agree. It was too late to turn back now. She knew they would not forgive her for the embarrassment and take her back. Ana stared blankly at the judge.

"You will report to the reform center."

A juvenile detention center? Why? She hadn't done anything!

"No, please, señor," Ana pleaded. "Please."

The judge did not look at her. Instead, he reached for the folder containing the details of the next case.

45

After dinner that night, Ana carried everything she owned in a grocery bag as she entered the reform center. She was given a cardboard box and told to store her personal items there. A tall woman with long black hair and severe eyes handed Ana a T-shirt and cotton shorts.

"This is your uniform," she said without smiling. "You will wear it every day."

Ana looked around. The building was an old one that had been converted into a reform home and orphanage. The facility consisted of three connected structures, one for small children, another for teenage girls, and a third for teenage boys. The walls were painted bright shades of coral and turquoise, but Ana saw everything as though she were looking through a gray rain cloud.

The guard led Ana to the girls' dormitory, where about twenty girls slept in rows of beds. There was no air-conditioning or fan; the stale, hot air hung in the room.

The guard unlocked the door, which looked like the metal bars of a prison cell. She held it open, and Ana passed through. The guard locked the door behind her saying, "The last row."

The bathroom was in the same room. The stalls had no doors, no privacy. No one spoke to her, so Ana suffered her humiliation in silence. She put on a mask of bravery and indifference, as if she had been in tougher situations in the past. She didn't want to let anyone sense her weakness and fear.

Ana found her way to her bed and climbed on the mattress, which felt like it had been filled with small stones. She cried silently in the hot, dark room. It was like being in hell—not the fiery red hell of the Bible, but a drab, colorless one. *I am in prison*, she thought. *What am I doing in this place?*

46

An alarm sounded at five in the morning. The sky was still black when the girls were directed outside and told to run ten laps around a large field. As the sun rose over the hills, they were divided into groups and told to pull weeds in the yard surrounding the buildings.

"What's your name?" a girl a bit younger than Ana asked without smiling.

"Ana."

"I'm Pilar."

While they worked, they talked a little about themselves. Pilar came from a small town in the mountains. She had been at the center for about six months, since just before her thirteenth birthday.

"You'll get used to it," Pilar said.

At seven o'clock, another alarm sounded and

breakfast was served in the large cafeteria. Ana was hungry, but she ate very little of her first meal: leftover bread so hard and stale that she knew she could hurt someone with it if she threw it hard enough.

After breakfast, Ana and Pilar sat together in the garden, watching the other girls play soccer. Precisely at noon, another alarm rang out, calling them to lunch, an unsatisfying combination of boiled chicken necks and overcooked yellow rice. Ana thought it looked like animal feed, so she refused to eat it.

In the afternoon, two women from one of the local churches came by to pray with the girls and give them a lesson in scripture. Ana listened politely, but she didn't say much.

Dinner looked like leftovers from lunch. Afterward, the girls who had behaved well during the day had the privilege to watch thirty minutes of television in a communal room before they went back to the dorm to sleep.

Ana did not want to sit with the other girls. She returned to the room early and pulled out her box of possessions. She dug to the bottom and found her picture of Mamá, as well as more recent photos of Papá, Isabel, and Yolanda. She looked at them and thought to herself, *I don't belong here.*

When she heard someone coming, she shoved the photos under her bed and pretended she was sleeping. She didn't want to share them with anyone; she wanted to keep that part of herself private.

47

In the morning, Ana and Pilar paired off again, this time pulling weeds in the garden behind the children's wing. Ana slipped on a pair of work gloves and began yanking weeds out of the dry soil. She dug down into the earth to pull the weeds by the roots, while Pilar snapped the stems at ground level.

"So, why are you in here?" Ana asked Pilar. Ana didn't want to push for too much information, but she thought that the sooner she could learn about the various personalities she was living with, the easier it would be to survive.

"I got caught," Pilar responded vaguely.

Ana waited for more.

"Working," Pilar added. Then Ana understood. She knew that each of the girls at the center lived with her own secrets. Some were drug users; some had been kicked out of their homes by parents and guardians; some, like Pilar, believed their only way to survive was to sell sex on the streets. Others, like Ana, were sent to the center because they had nowhere else to go.

"You were forced to become a prostitute?" Ana asked incredulously.

"Amiga, don't be stupid. I had to. Those men, those animals paid me and that was the only way I could eat."

"I didn't mean it that way," Ana said. "It's just, I mean, you're so young."

"I was twelve," Pilar whispered. "My mom kicked me out of the house and I was taken in by someone who said he was going to help me. He was a liar."

Pilar's tone was flat and expressionless; she spoke as if her shame and heartache had hardened into a shell that deflected all emotion. "I needed the money."

Ana tried not to be judgmental. She thought about telling Pilar that she, too, knew what it felt like to be held down by the grimy hand of an older man, but she wasn't ready to tell her the truth. Ana knew that Pilar's life held as much shame as her own, so she changed the subject.

Over time, Ana learned that other girls at the center had also worked the streets. At first Ana couldn't believe that any girl would be forced into selling herself for five or ten dollars, but then she thought about her own secrets and how easy it was for her to box up these parts of her life, separating them so that she could deny that they were part of her at all.

48

Ana was afraid of telling any of the girls too much about herself. She rarely spoke to anyone except Pilar.

A month after she entered the reform center, a lady with a sweet face motioned to her after lunch and asked her to come with her to her office.

As they sat facing each other, Ana knew who this was. She was expecting her, just not this soon.

"I'm María, your psychologist," the lady said.

Ana was angry. She knew that everyone in the center had to meet twice a week with a psychologist, but Ana hoped that this moment would never come. She didn't want to tell this stranger about her life, what she held inside.

"Ana, I'm here to be your friend, to help you," María said after a couple minutes of silence. "I know that you've experienced pain and sadness in your life.

I want to help you learn to express—"

"How do you know what I've experienced? You know nothing about me," Ana spat sharply.

"I want to get to know you. We can take our time," María continued.

Ana ignored her and they sat in silence for the twenty minutes remaining in their session.

49

The guards and María knew Ana was HIV-positive, but she told no one else in the center because she thought they would beat or harass her if they knew.

Every morning after breakfast and every night after dinner, one of the guards or María escorted Ana to the administrative office and handed her the white pills. When people asked where she was going, Ana told them she was going to get dessert. She knew they didn't believe her, but she didn't care what they thought she was doing, as long as they didn't know the truth.

Slowly, Ana began to trust María; she appreciated that María didn't tell any of the other girls that Ana had HIV. She became accustomed to seeing María every Wednesday and Friday morning, and the tension in their relationship began to peel away. At first they talked about pleasant things: school, friends, and Isabel.

As the weeks passed, Ana told María *all* of her secrets: the abuse she suffered from her abuela, her aunt, and Ernesto. Her face burned with shame when she told her the details of the night that Ernesto pinned her down. María told her that she had nothing to be ashamed of; it was not her fault.

Ana felt herself changing with María's help. She began to learn how to express her pain and how to forgive. She left the sessions feeling lighter, happier.

50

As Ana came out of her shell, she began to mix with the others and, like all the girls, looked forward to seeing the boys during meals. Ana thought about boys—a lot—but she didn't worry about spreading HIV, because she did not have intimate contact with them. The only time the boys and girls were in the same room was during mealtime, when they were under the vigilant eyes of the guards. Without speaking, the girls made a game of walking back and forth from the food line while trying to get the attention of the boy they liked.

Ana amused herself by writing notes to her boyfriend José. She had spoken to him briefly a couple of times when the guards weren't watching. She didn't want to be caught and lose television time or, worse, be locked in the punishment cell. But passing notes to José kept Ana from feeling bored and suffocated.

Besides, José was tall and handsome.

Ana dropped a note on his table as she passed on the way to the cafeteria line. She felt a surge of excitement when he looked up at her and smiled.

51

In March, when the academic year started, Ana was overjoyed to learn that she would be able to return to school. She would transfer to a school closer to the center for eighth grade. The school days were divided into morning and afternoon shifts because of over-crowding; Ana would attend the afternoon session, so a bus would arrive at the center at noon every day to pick her up.

Ana wished she could return to school with Yolanda and Señor García, but she had no choice except to start over at a new school. She missed them. She had gotten many letters from Yolanda and her mom at the beginning, but not so many anymore. She was irri-tated that the strict rules of the center prevented non–family members from visiting. Señor García had also sent her several letters and care packages. In one letter he told Ana that she was smart and capable, that he had confidence in her abilities and intelligence. Ana wanted to work hard and earn a scholarship to the university. This would please Señor García, and she desperately wanted to make someone proud.

52

At the center, nothing changed but the seasons. The daily routine created a rhythm that helped pass the time, as the weeks turned into months. Isabel visited once or twice, but it was difficult for her to find the seventy-five cents needed for bus fare and to figure out the transfers and bus schedules necessary to travel from one side of the city to the other. Ana felt abandoned and alone.

On most days, Ana put on a tough exterior and thought of herself as independent. As her quinceañera, her "sweet fifteenth" birthday, approached, she longed to celebrate with her family. In Latin American cultures, a quinceañera marks a milestone: It is the day a girl is recognized by society as a woman. Ana considered her quinceañera one of the most important days in her life, a day that was supposed to be filled with tradition and family.

Several times a year, the women from the church arranged parties for the girls celebrating their quinceañeras. There was so little to look forward to in the center that Ana placed special meaning on this day; she counted down the days by marking Xs on the calendar she kept next to her bed.

On the morning of her birthday, when the five o'clock buzzer sounded, Ana jumped to her feet, eager for the day to begin. Instead of working outside, Ana showered and dressed in her street clothes; two of the women from church came and drove her to a beauty salon. Ana had never been to a real salon before; she admired the colorful bottles of shampoo and marveled at the hair combs, clips, and ribbons on display. On this day, all of the colors she saw seemed more vibrant, from the lime and jade green palm trees to the bright red and blue swing sets she passed in the park.

Ana stared at her reflection in the mirror. She blew a kiss to herself playfully. Then she stepped closer and examined her face. She stared intently into her dark brown eyes and lost herself for a moment. She saw beyond what the rest of the world saw; for just a second, she felt she saw herself as she really was—alone, and vulnerable—and this frightened her. She looked away, blinked her eyes, and then blew another kiss.

One of the attendants washed and conditioned her lush black hair. Then a stylist blow-dried her curls into smooth waves.

When Ana's hair was finished, a beautician plucked her thick eyebrows into gentle arches. She smoothed on a thin layer of foundation, applied coral shadow to her eyelids and a soft, shell color on her cheeks. She brushed on a thin coat of mascara and finished by painting her lips pink, the color of a sunset.

When Ana looked in the mirror, she saw a beautiful girl. For the first time since she had been at the center, Ana felt attractive and alive.

When Ana returned to the facility in the early afternoon, María stopped her and said, "Qué linda, how beautiful you look." She took Ana into the administration building and went to a closet in the back room. She came out holding a magnificent white dress adorned with melon-colored flowers and tiny pearls. Passing the dress to Ana, she said, "I think you would look lovely in this."

Ana slipped into the gown, and María placed a pearl tiara gently into her hair. She felt just as she had when she celebrated her first communion two years before. But in that moment, Ana was homesick. More than anything else, she wished that Isabel—and maybe even her abuela—could celebrate this day with her.

53

Everyone was in the cafeteria for the party when Ana entered the room. The room had been transformed. The walls, a seafoam blue, reminded her of the color of the Caribbean Ocean. Coral balloons hung above the stage at the front of the room, and white spirals of crepe paper floated like jellyfish from the ceiling. Rows of chairs faced the stage, where the ceremony would be held.

Ana walked down the aisle escorted by one of the boys. Some of her friends walked behind her as her court. She glanced over at José and found him staring at her, mesmerized.

Ana stood on the stage as a priest said a special Mass dedicated to her transition from childhood to womanhood. He explained that she wore a tiara because she was a princess in the eyes of God.

Ana's Story

After the ceremony, Ana waltzed with her escort to traditional music blasting from a boom box onstage. The day ended with Ana's friends surrounding her and singing "Feliz cumpleaños" before she sliced her pink birthday cake.

54

The week after Ana's quinceañera, José left the center. One day he was sitting at dinner, trading flirtatious grins with Ana from a table across the room; the next day he was gone, without a warning or a good-bye.

"Where is José?" Ana asked one of the other boys when she got up to scrape her plate over the garbage can.

"He's gone," came the reply. "I guess he went home."

That was it.

During the year she spent at the center, Ana had seen many people come and go. Some of the wild, tough girls who couldn't stand the strict guidelines ran away; some were transferred to other facilities; some were lucky enough to have families who eventually brought them home.

Ana wasn't really upset that José had left. She had

enjoyed his sugary words, words like candy—"Mi amor, you are the most beautiful girl in the room, like a dark angel"—but she never really knew him.

With José gone, what Ana missed most was the distraction he had offered.

55

A few weeks later, a group from the church came to teach a volleyball clinic to the teens in the yard of the center. Ana liked the competitiveness of volleyball; she welcomed the change of pace—and the chance to mix with the boys.

Ana practiced her serve for a few minutes, then went through the first series of drills on setting the ball. The entire time, her attention was divided between the game and the boys.

"Hey, Ricardo, nice shot," she said, smiling.

"You, too," he said.

Ana attracted attention from those around her by focusing on one person at a time. She didn't look away when someone saw her gazing; she wasn't afraid to let someone know she was looking.

Ana was also friendly with those who had a

harder time fitting in. She often brought others into the games or sometimes left the match to go talk to someone.

Ana spotted a new boy sitting alone under a tree. His skin was tanned, and the soccer jersey he wore underscored his slight, hunched frame.

When Ana tired of volleyball, she walked over and sat down next to him.

"Hey, you're new," Ana said.

"Sí," the boy said, smiling but not looking at Ana.

"I'm Ana."

"I'm Berto," he said, glancing up at her. His eyes were chocolate brown, much like her own.

Ana immediately liked Berto. She felt more comfortable with his gentle quietness than the bravado of other boys, who strutted and showed off for her. Maybe he could be a real friend.

"So, what brings you here?" Ana asked, trying to make Berto feel at ease.

He shrugged.

Berto's shyness emboldened Ana.

"I'm here because no one wants me," she said dramatically, somewhat surprised by her own honesty.

"Then I guess we have something in common," Berto replied quietly.

The two remained under the tree, looking out at the volleyball game rather than at each other, speaking easily about the past. Ana also felt comfortable when the conversation stopped; they both knew how to enjoy a moment of peaceful silence. Ana learned that they were both orphans, unwanted by other family members.

"How did your parents die?" Ana asked.

"They were sick," Berto said.

"Mine, too."

56

Ana felt closer to Berto than anyone she knew except for Isabel, whom she had not seen in months. Although she hadn't told Berto her secrets, she somehow felt that he would understand if she ever did.

Ana passed him notes at dinner. At first she wrote about mundane things like the food in the cafeteria and the names she used to describe the guards, but over time they started asking each other more serious questions.

Once, Berto wrote, "Where do you go after dinner each night?"

Ana, not sure if she was being reckless or courageous, replied, "This is a secret. I am infected with HIV. In the evenings, I go and take my medicine." Before she could change her mind, Ana slipped the note to Berto and kept walking out of the cafeteria and back to her bed in the girls' dorm.

Ana worried that her friendship with Berto would be over or, worse, that he would tell the others. She had to wait until the following day at breakfast to find out what he would do.

57

Ana's heart pounded as she entered the cafeteria for breakfast. She glanced over the room, trying not to be obvious, but hoping to spot Berto and get a smile or some sign of acknowledgment that would show her if he accepted her for who she was.

She saw only the back of his head.

Ana went through the cafeteria line and then had to walk across the room to the girls' tables. She held her head high and walked quickly past his table. At the last second, she glanced in his direction and saw him looking at her, smiling. This time he held her gaze, his eyes promising that he would not betray her.

It was Berto's turn to slip a note to Ana.

She went back to the dorm alone and pulled out the slip of paper that Berto had folded in half, and in half again.

He had written, "I have it, too."

58

Ana felt all of the tension she had carried for the previous twenty-four hours drain away. She had been accepted; she was happy that she could accept him in return. Ana felt a bond with Berto that she had never felt with another boy, a bond built on trust and friendship.

Lying in bed, Ana wondered whether everything was happening to her for a reason. Maybe she had been in this place just so that this moment would occur; maybe God sent her Berto, a real friend, as a sign that she had been alone long enough.

59

Two days later, Berto was gone.

Like José, he was present in the morning at breakfast, and he had disappeared by lunch.

Ana looked for Berto in the cafeteria during lunch, but she didn't see him. She wondered if he hadn't felt well and stayed back in his room. She didn't worry, since she had no reason to think that he was going anywhere.

She chatted with her friends throughout lunch, and just before she got up to clear her plate, one of Berto's roommates passed her a note. Ana slipped it in her pocket and went to the restroom so she could read it in private.

> *Ana,*
> *I'm leaving this place. I'm being transferred to a home for people like us. I'll try to get them to take you. I won't forget you. Ever.*

Ana was confused. Could Berto actually be gone? She didn't understand where he went or why. They were just getting started; she had so much more to tell him.

Ana went to the administration office and found one of the guards sitting at a desk doing paperwork.

"Where did Berto go?" Ana asked.

"Who?"

"Berto. The boy who came two weeks ago."

"Oh, him," the guard said. "Yes, he's gone, and you don't need to worry about where he went." Just like that, Berto had disappeared from her life.

60

Ana wanted to forget Berto, but she couldn't. She wanted to regret telling him her secret, but she didn't. Ana tried to convince herself that knowing him didn't matter, but her heart never let him go.

With Berto gone, the days at the center dragged. Ana feared that she would never escape the monotony of her life confined to the concrete box she now lived in. When she became angry, she used her sessions with María to discuss her frustrations and pain. She realized that her emotions didn't have the power to control her anymore. This made her feel stronger and more free.

61

A few weeks later, a woman stopped by the administration office. Ana sat on her bed, weary and tired. From down the hall, she thought she heard the guard mention her name.

She heard footsteps; then the guard said, "Ana, gather your stuff. You're being transferred."

She thought of José and Berto; this time it was her turn to disappear.

Ana had no idea where she was going. Would she go home with Isabel, who was now living with her godfather? Would she live with her favorite aunt, Aída?

Ana pulled the box from under her bed. The jeans she wore when she had arrived no longer fit. Even though she was a year older, she was thinner from eating very little. She had to wear the uniform she had on. She didn't care if she said good-bye to the other girls; Pilar, her closest friend, had left long before. Ana had now been at the center longer than any of the other girls in her dorm. But she wished she could have said good-bye to María, who was gone for the day. So Ana scribbled her a quick note.

"I'm ready," Ana said to the woman standing next to the guard, waiting to take her to her new home, wherever that was this time.

62

Ana didn't say anything as she put her box in the trunk of the car and then opened the passenger door.

"I'm Silvia," said the woman, climbing into the driver's seat. "I work at the Rosa Mística, your new hogar, your new home."

Ana's heart dropped. She wasn't going home to be with Isabel.

"You're now old enough to come to our facility, which is one of the few group homes for people with HIV/AIDS," Silvia said.

Ana's head snapped up. How could this stranger know her secret?

"It's okay, Ana," Silvia said warmly. "Everyone at the hogar has HIV or AIDS."

When they arrived at the hogar, Silvia led Ana through two large metal doors into a covered courtyard filled with blossoming tropical plants. Fuchsia bougain-villea climbed a trellis along one wall, and bright orange bird of paradise grew along the perimeter of the garden. Paintings of saints hung on the stucco walls, protecting those who lived within the gates.

Ana looked around and saw about ten or twelve men and women sitting in smaller groups, talking, sewing, and playing cards. A thin old man with frizzy gray hair sat in a rocking chair listening to a soccer game on an old portable radio. Two middle-aged women sat together and knitted.

In the far corner a young man and a teenage boy played checkers. They laughed quietly as one gained an advantage. The boy sitting with his back to her wore a large white T-shirt that was too big for his small body; his hair was buzzed short, like mowed grass. The older one nodded in her direction, and then the young man turned to look.

Ana stopped and her mouth dropped. Looking at her from across the courtyard was Berto, a smile on his face.

"Berto!" Ana cried out. "What are you doing here?"

"I told you I would take you to a better place," he said, looking at her shyly.

"Berto shared your name with us," Silvia said. "We

reviewed your file at the center and decided that this would be a more comfortable home for you."

Ana couldn't speak. So this is what he meant in his note to her. She hadn't understood because she had never heard about a home for people living with HIV/AIDS. In her experience, people with HIV/AIDS were not welcomed anywhere. But they were welcomed here.

63

At her first family meal at the hogar, Ana sat at a long wooden table with all of the residents. Silvia and Pablo, the administrators, did not have HIV/AIDS, but they lived in the home and managed the facility. Before eating, everyone around the table held hands and prayed.

"Amén," they all said at the end of the prayer.

Ana was amazed by the quality and freshness of the food. She ate a casserole of chicken and rice, along with fresh vegetables and tomato soup. She took special note of the bright colors on the table—green, yellow, orange, red—so different from the beige mush she was accustomed to at the center.

"Is the food always like this?" Ana asked Berto, who was seated next to her.

"Even better for Sunday breakfast," he said after

swallowing. Berto never lifted his eyes from his plate; Ana remembered the shyness that she had found so refreshing when she first sat with Berto under the tree at the center.

Berto barely had a chance to speak anyway. Around the table, everyone asked questions of Ana and told her the stories of their lives—where they were from, how long they had lived in this home—and some told her how they had been infected with HIV/AIDS. These words were not whispered with shame but stated as fact. "I'm María and I have been living with AIDS for fifteen years," said one of the middle-aged women who had been knitting earlier. "I was infected by my husband, who was injecting drugs."

Ana had never imagined such openness about AIDS. At this table, there was a group of people doing their best to live with HIV/AIDS without shame, blame, or fear. She didn't need to hide her pills or sneak away to take them in private. At the end of the meal, one of the women said, "Okay, vamos, let's go, let's take our medicine."

"I call it my dessert," said Ana, and everyone laughed. Everyone at the table reached for the pills sitting next to their plates.

64

After dinner, Silvia showed Ana to her bedroom. All of the residents slept in rooms with doors that faced a common courtyard. Ana would sleep in a large room with four other women. Some residents, including Berto, had private rooms. The women's quarters were on one side of the courtyard, the men's on the other.

Ana liked the soft lavender color on the bedroom walls. Silvia gave Ana clean sheets for her bed. Hers was a twin bed in the corner of the room, near the door.

Since Ana didn't have many clothes, Silvia took her to a large closet filled with hand-me-downs and cast-offs from various shelters. Silvia told Ana to go through the boxes and look for anything she liked that might fit. Ana found pink T-shirts, jean shorts, a pair of gold sandals that laced up her calves, a white jean skirt, and a red tank top. Ana had always loved choosing outfits;

she hadn't been able to wear anything but the regulation center shorts and T-shirts for nearly two years.

Ana took her new clothes back to her room and tucked them into a drawer—*her* drawer. She unpacked the cardboard box, carefully removing the photocopy of her mother and the photographs of Papá, Isabel, and Yolanda.

Ana pinned the images to the wall next to her bed, placing her mother's in the center. She created a collage of the people of her past. She could stare at the pictures from her bed, just as she did when she was a little girl living at her abuela's house.

65

At fifteen, Ana and Berto were by far the youngest residents at the hogar. No one was surprised when they became instant partners, doing everything together. Ana and Berto ate breakfast together; then they completed their morning chores, which consisted of doing the dishes, mopping the kitchen floor, or collecting the laundry.

After lunch, they sat together in front of a TV in Berto's room watching telenovelas and sharing the stories of their lives.

Berto told Ana of an early childhood that was similar to her own. He was an orphan who never knew his mamá or papá. He lived with his aunt, who beat him and ridiculed him for the disease he was born with, telling him he was weak, sick, disgusting, and filthy. When Berto was twelve years old, he ran away. He had been the same age as Ana when she left her abuela's house.

At that point, his story took a sharper turn. Berto dropped out of the sixth grade and lived on the street with a group of young boys, robbing grocery stores and stealing cars to get by. When he was fifteen years old, he was caught by the police and brought into the juvenile detention center. Like two streams, Ana's and Berto's stories merged into one when they met at the center.

Berto narrated his story as an observer, clearly but without much emotion. She understood that the real feeling lay beyond the words, underneath the facts, in that place where the feelings were hidden. Ana knew Berto wasn't trying to be tough or to impress her; she knew because she told her stories in the same way. It was easier not to be emotional, not to be involved. Then it didn't hurt so much.

66

All of the residents at the hogar were invited to go to meetings of an HIV/AIDS support group. Ana went to her first meeting a month after she arrived at the hogar, where she met Sara, the director of the program.

"The purpose of the meetings is to educate ourselves about the ways we can stay healthy," said Sara in a calm, soothing voice. "We meet twice a week to discuss the importance of good nutrition, of taking our medicines, and of supporting each other."

Ana had gotten the chance to learn about HIV/AIDS before, but she had never listened as carefully as she did now. This was different from when she was a young girl in school, only partially hearing the teacher because she had been so nervous and afraid that someone would discover her secret. But now she didn't have to worry about that; she felt comfortable listening and asking questions.

"There are ways you can help yourself stay healthy," said Sara, "and you need to learn how to prevent the spread of the infection."

Ana focused on every word. Before the meeting, she hadn't completely understood how the virus worked to weaken her immune system. She didn't appreciate the importance of eating healthy foods to keep her body strong enough to control the virus. She now understood how important the use of condoms is not only to prevent pregnancy but also to prevent the spread of HIV/AIDS during sex.

That night, Ana sat on the couch staring at Berto.

"What are you thinking about, guapa?" Berto asked casually. Ana liked that he called her beautiful.

"The meeting," Ana said. "I've spent my whole life avoiding talking about HIV/AIDS and now I really want to talk about it."

"I understand," Berto said. "I like the meetings too. They're the closest thing I have to school."

Ana and Berto tried to turn their attention to the television, but they were both lost in their own thoughts. Berto broke the silence. "Ana, do you ever think about dying?"

"No," Ana said quickly. "Don't be morbid. Besides,

everyone dies. I prefer to think about living."

Ana leaned over and kissed Berto on the cheek and went back to her room. She wanted some time alone.

Ana sat on the bed, letting her thoughts wander. She considered Berto's question. Ana decided that she preferred to ignore death, as if it were a pesky bug in the corner of the room. Many people she loved had died—her mamá, her papá, her baby sister, friends from the hospital. In the last month, two people had moved from the hogar to the hospital, and she didn't expect to see either one of them again.

Ana knew she lived in denial. She knew she could die from HIV/AIDS, but she looked healthy and felt fine, and she didn't want to waste her time thinking about being sick. She had always been diligent about taking her medicine, and she rarely suffered from colds or the flu.

Ana stared at the image of her mamá on the wall and thought about how much the medicine and treatment for AIDS had changed since Mamá died twelve years before. Ana now knew that many of the drugs used to treat HIV/AIDS had not been as widely available and effective when her mother, sister, and father had died. At the meeting, Sara said that the drugs for HIV/AIDS were improving all the time and that,

155

while it didn't look like there would be a cure for AIDS anytime in the near future, the medicines currently available could help Ana stay healthy for a long time, as long as she took them every day.

Ana thought some more and then decided: No, she really didn't fear death, but she respected death. She accepted that death was waiting for her, but she had no intention of giving in; she planned to fight it, and the best way she could do that was to *live*. She was beginning to understand, though, that she needed to live responsibly.

67

Ana and Berto sat together on the couch in the community room every evening and watched movies. They always sat side by side, close enough for their knees to bump but far enough away so no one walking in would think that they were interrupting anything. Ana liked feeling the warmth of Berto's skin.

One night when Berto and Ana were the only two in the room, when the movie was over and the final credits were scrolling across the screen, Berto leaned over and whispered into Ana's ear: "Me gustas."

Ana trembled. She felt the words like a flush through her body. Berto had said, "I like you." These three words changed everything for Ana.

68

In the morning, Ana smiled at Berto when she sat down for breakfast. She wore the mandatory school uniform: a white collared shirt and a navy blue pleated skirt. Her hair was woven into a long, shiny braid.

"This is a big day," Ana said to Silvia while putting some warm plantains on her plate. "Ninth grade."

Ana had transferred to a new school; she needed only two years to graduate from secondary school.

"I hate first days," she said. "I'm always so nervous."

Berto wasn't able to go to school, but he hoped to return when he felt better. He had dropped out at age twelve, when he ran away from home.

Ana finished her breakfast and said good-bye. Her eyes lingered on Berto, and she smiled. She then rushed off to wait for the bus outside the hogar.

When she returned, Berto was waiting for her.

"Let's go for a walk," he said, eager to get outside.

They walked through the neighborhood, talking about Ana's classes and some of the girls she ate with in the cafeteria. Ana appreciated having a chance to talk about her day with someone who really wanted to listen.

A few blocks from the hogar, they sat on a bench in a park. Berto reached up and gently stroked Ana's long black hair. He leaned toward her, and they shared a tender kiss. Ana had kissed other boys before, but she had never felt a connection like this; shivers ran up her spine, and her mouth curved into a perfect smile.

69

For the next several months, Ana returned from school and spent every afternoon with Berto, walking through the barrio, looking in shops, watching movies at the hogar. Once, Silvia and Pablo took all the residents to the beach. She and Berto swam in the salty

waves and danced to Shakira on the radio as the sun set behind the ocean.

Ana considered Berto her novio, her boyfriend, although they tried not to act like a couple when they were back at the hogar. They didn't think that their relationship violated any rules, but they weren't sure and didn't want Silvia or Pablo to start watching them closely. So they kept their relationship a secret.

Ana felt connected to Berto; she trusted him more than anyone except Isabel. She could not imagine either one of them deliberately doing anything to hurt her. Berto didn't yell or swear at her; he held her hand when they walked together; every day he told her that he loved her and needed her.

Some evenings, Ana slipped into Berto's bedroom to watch television instead of watching in the common room. They usually watched comedies or soap operas, but one night they turned on *Law & Order*. In this episode, a middle-aged psychopath had attacked a young girl, and the detectives were trying to solve the case.

"Why do you want to watch this trash?" Ana asked, feeling uncomfortable because she had been reminded of Ernesto.

"Come on, it's good," Berto said. "Are you scared, guapa?" he teased, tickling Ana under her arms.

Ana didn't want to explain that the show terrified her. She snuggled up to Berto, but she tried not to look at the screen. She counted the number of tiles on the floor and thought of a topic for an upcoming religion project, but the scene on the television kept drawing her back.

As Ana watched the grainy black-and-white television, she became more and more tense. She had tried to forget Ernesto, but like a dust storm this program stirred up old memories. Memories of that night—Ernesto's eyes, his grubby hands, her inability to scream—flashed through her mind.

"What's wrong?" Berto asked.

"Oh, nada, nothing," she replied. This was one secret she had kept from him; the shame still haunted her.

"I know something is wrong," Berto said, his voice warm and soft. "It's okay, you can trust me."

Ana looked at Berto, and she felt safe and loved; she wanted to trust him completely. She told him about the horrific night years before when Ernesto came into her room. At first the words came out robotically, as if she didn't feel their full meaning. But as the story continued, she broke down and began to sob.

"Ana, it's all right," Berto said, wrapping his arms around her. "I'm here for you."

She shook her head no.

Ana drew a deep breath and said, "It's my fault."

"No, guapa, it's not," Berto offered. "You didn't do anything. Why should you feel bad for something that animal did to you?"

Ana sat up, looked him in the eye, and said between hiccuplike gasps, "I didn't protect mi hermana. I didn't protect Isabel." Berto couldn't comfort her, but he held her and that was enough.

70

Ana hadn't expected to live in a home with a makeshift family of people living with HIV/AIDS. She hadn't expected to find someone she trusted completely. Most of all, she hadn't expected to fall in love with Berto.

After the night that Ana revealed all of her secrets to Berto, there was nothing that separated them. He knew everything about her, and still he loved her. Ana let her guard down with Berto, making their love stronger in a way that she could not have imagined.

The next Sunday, Ana and Berto ate breakfast together and attended the Mass that was offered in the courtyard of the hogar. Ana could think of no place she would rather be than in the sanctuary of that garden, standing next to Berto, singing joyful songs. She had opened herself completely to him, and her heart was no longer weighed down by her secrets.

After the service, Silvia and Pablo took most of the residents to the supermarket and to run other errands. Ana and Berto stayed behind.

The hogar was quiet. The air smelled like cut grass. Gold afternoon sunlight filtered from the hallway into Berto's room. Ana and Berto sat next to each other on the couch, watching television and listening to one another breathe.

They began kissing. Berto ran his fingers through Ana's long, wavy hair. She looked into his eyes and saw pleasure and desire.

"Berto, are you sure we should do this?" Ana asked between kisses, sensing that they were about to take things one step further. She felt no fear, only love.

"Te quiéro, guapa, I love you," he said gently. Ana's heart felt overcome with love, but she wanted to be safe.

"Do you have any condoms?" Ana asked, but it was all happening too fast. "We should use condoms," she said, as if trying to convince herself as well as Berto.

"I'll get some tomorrow," he said. This time, it was too late.

71

Ana spent her days in school and her afternoons with Berto. At night, when the house was dark and everyone had gone to sleep, Ana snuck through the courtyard to Berto's bedroom and they made love. They used condoms every night except the first.

72

On most mornings, Ana awoke at five-thirty to dress and eat breakfast before the bus arrived. She usually stole a moment or two to look at the picture of her mamá on the wall, silently telling her about what was going on in her life. Ana told her mamá about her feelings for Berto and how he had written her a love poem. She liked to think her mamá would be happy for her.

But one morning, Ana felt nauseous, as if she had just gotten off one of the spinning carnival rides she used to go on with Papá. She jumped out of bed and vomited.

For the next several weeks, Ana was queasy and sick almost every morning, and she felt tired and feverish through the day.

At first, Ana feared that she could be pregnant, but she had had her period a couple of weeks before, though it was lighter than usual, so she ruled out pregnancy.

"I think I have some sort of stomach illness," Ana told Silvia one morning at breakfast. "I am not sure what it is, but I wake up nauseous every morning."

"You need to see a doctor," Silvia said without alarm. "I'll take you after school." Silvia spent a lot of time with the residents living with HIV/AIDS, so she wasn't distressed by what she suspected was a mild stomach bug. After all, Ana seemed to shake the illness by midmorning, and it hadn't interfered with her ability to go to school.

Silvia took Ana to the hospital after school. Ana wasn't at all nervous; she spent a lot of time there picking up her HIV/AIDS medications and visiting friends from the hogar.

Silvia waited in the reception area while Ana went in to see the doctor.

"Hello, Ana, I'm your doctor," a young woman said as she came in. "First, how old are you?"

"I'm sixteen," Ana replied while the doctor took notes on a brown clipboard.

"And what seems to be the problem?"

Ana told her about the nausea and vomiting.

"When was your last period?" the doctor asked.

"I'm not exactly sure, but it was a couple of weeks ago," Ana said.

"All right, then I'm going to do an ultrasound to see what the problem is," the doctor said.

Ana lay back on the exam table and rested her head on a tiny pillow on one end. The room felt cold and drafty. The doctor rubbed jelly on Ana's stomach and then began the ultrasound. When the doctor turned off the machine, she lent Ana a hand so that she could sit up.

"Ana, you aren't sick," the doctor said.

"Oh, thank God," Ana said, letting out a deep breath. She had been thinking about her father and his illness, the months he spent wasting away.

"You are four months pregnant," the doctor added.

"No," Ana said, "I had my period." She was sure that something must be wrong.

"Sometimes women have spotting early in their pregnancy during the time they would normally have their period," the doctor explained. "That must be what you experienced, because you *are* pregnant."

Ana panicked. The room began to spin, and she thought she was going to be sick. Her mind raced: How could she finish school? What would Berto think? How could she take care of a baby?

169

And then she felt numb: What if her baby had HIV?

She tried to ask the doctor, "Will my baby . . . will my baby have . . ." She couldn't continue. She felt suffocated and couldn't catch her breath.

"Ana, calm down," the doctor said. "You will be okay, and your baby should be okay. If you take medication and follow other precautions while you are pregnant, there is a very good chance your baby will be perfectly healthy."

"I can't believe it," Ana said over and over like a scratched CD.

73

When the doctor left the room, Ana put on her clothes and washed her face. She looked up at her reflection in the mirror above the sink and thought, *You're going to be a mamá.*

She felt that someone else was looking back at her. She was only sixteen years old, too young to have a baby. Still, once the doctor told her she was pregnant, she could begin to feel the life inside her. She stared at the person in the mirror again, and for a second she thought she saw her mother looking back. Ana's mother had been sixteen when Ana was born.

"Mamá," Ana said to her reflection, "what am I going to do?"

Ana shook her head as if she were trying to awaken from a dream. She opened the door and walked back to the waiting room.

"I'm fine," Ana told Silvia, who had been waiting for almost two hours. "Let's go home."

Silvia didn't press for details. "I'm glad you're feeling better," she said, giving Ana the same privacy that she allowed all the people living in the hogar.

Ana didn't speak on the way home. When they arrived, Ana said, "Thanks for the ride. I've got to get started on my homework." She went back to her room, nestled under the comfort of her sheets, and fell asleep.

74

After dinner that evening, Ana walked down to Berto's room, knocked on the door, and went inside.

Ana felt nervous, like she was moving in slow motion.

"Hey there," Berto said, clearly glad to see her.

For no reason—and for every reason—Ana began to laugh. She couldn't stop. The more she tried to control herself, the more absurd she felt and the harder she laughed.

"What's so funny? What has happened to you?" Berto asked.

She laughed harder, tears streaming down her face, then said, "Berto, you're going to be a father." She gasped for breath and said again, "You are going to be a papá."

Berto's face became serious. "Is this true? Ana, is this for real?"

Ana nodded her head, rapidly sobering up as she felt the significance of what she was saying. She stopped laughing and asked, "Berto, now what are we going to do?"

75

After Ana told Berto, he started to laugh, too, only his was joyful rather than nervous laughter.

"We're having a baby," he said, adjusting to the idea. "We're having a baby."

Berto's enthusiasm comforted her like a warm blanket. He kissed the top of her head and stroked her hair gently.

"We're going to have to tell Silvia and Pablo," Berto said.

"I know," Ana said, but she was afraid.

The following morning, Ana asked Silvia and Pablo if she and Berto could speak to them in private. All four sat at the kitchen table after everyone had cleared the breakfast dishes.

"We have something to tell you," Ana started. She looked at Berto for assistance, but he was looking out the window. She would have to be the strong one.

"This is difficult to say," she started.

"Just say it, Ana," Silvia said.

"I have never seen you look so serious, guapa," Pablo joked.

"I am pregnant. I am pregnant, and Berto is the baby's father." Ana took a deep breath; she felt her face flush.

"What? Oh, Ana, Berto," Silvia said. "How could you have done this?" Silvia asked, rubbing her hands against her temples. "You both are HIV-positive. You can make each other sicker."

Neither Ana nor Berto spoke.

Silvia drew a deep breath. "What were you thinking?" she asked angrily. "You shouldn't have been having sex at all—and certainly not without a condom."

"It was once," Ana said, defending herself, her face hot. "Once without a condom."

"Once was enough, Ana. And now your baby is also in danger. Now what?" Pablo asked. "This is a home for teenagers and adults. We can't keep a baby here. You're going to need to find another home, Ana."

Ana's heart stopped. She loved living in the hogar. It was the closest thing she had known to her dream home in the orchard. Where could she go? It had never occurred to her that she would have to leave the hogar, and especially Berto.

Ana began to sob.

"Calm down, Ana," Silvia said. "We will figure it out. We will figure this out."

76

In the next few weeks, Ana's nausea began to subside, but her emotions began to swing back and forth like a pendulum. Some days she was excited and euphoric—honored that God had chosen her to be a mother—and other days she was anxious and afraid. Some days she imagined that she could provide her child with the loving and stable home she had longed for during her own childhood; other days she feared that she would repeat the cycle of her past and that her baby could end up like her sister Lucía, who never made it home from the hospital. Ana vowed to do everything she could to prevent her baby from developing HIV/AIDS.

Ana had always been responsible about taking her medication, but she now understood that she needed to take her medication not just to protect herself but to protect her baby as well. Taking her medicine each day was the first thing she could do to offer her baby a good life. Every time she swallowed a pill, she thought to herself, *I'm doing this for you, mi niña*. Somehow, from the beginning, Ana knew she would have a girl.

77

At first, Ana didn't tell her friends that she was pregnant. When she was at school, she acted like a sixteen-year-old girl, concerned with homework and gossip. Sometimes, when she let her mind wander in class, she remembered the baby and smiled. No one had any idea that she had a new life inside her.

In a few weeks, Ana's skirt began to pull around her waist as her belly grew. She had lost some weight in the beginning of her pregnancy because she was sick so often, but she had made that up and more.

"Hey, chica, you're getting fat," one of her friends told her when they were waiting in line for lunch.

Instead of defending herself or offering a snide remark in response, Ana smiled.

Her friends noticed that rather than being insulted, Ana seemed to feel proud.

"What, are you pregnant?" asked one of her friends, laughing as she gently pulled the sleeve of her shirt.

Ana said nothing.

An astonished look passed over their faces, and the girls huddled together and whispered, "You are!" "Is it Berto?" "When will the baby come?"

Ana's friends had heard her talk nonstop about Berto, but they had never met him.

The girls spent the rest of the lunch hour trying to come up with names for the baby. Ana enjoyed the attention from her friends; for days, Ana and her baby were all anyone could talk about. She felt special and important. Ana also knew that she was lucky; many schools in her neighborhood would not allow pregnant students to stay enrolled.

Ana didn't know how much work a baby would be. She didn't worry about balancing her jobs as a mother and a student. At that moment, all she could focus on was her baby and how she would love her.

78

Ana went to school most days, but she did her assignments at home if she felt tired or nauseous. Berto got a job washing cars in the streets so that he would have money to buy Ana maternity shirts and clothes for the baby.

Berto worked hard, but his left hip hurt. It had given him trouble off and on for months, but the pain now felt like sharp gravel grinding into his joints. He went to a doctor, who told him he had an infection in his hip. The doctor gave him a cane to take some of the weight off when he was standing or walking.

Within a couple of weeks, Berto could no longer stand long enough to wash a car. His leg throbbed all the time, and he hobbled like an old man. He couldn't work anymore, and Ana worried about him and also whether he would ever be well enough to help her take care of their baby.

79

When she was seven months pregnant, Ana's family at the hogar threw a baby shower for her. Ana was still sure she was having a girl.

The residents of the hogar bought the baby a chest of drawers, a crib, a fan, and piles of tiny pink clothes, including handmade socks and a shirt. They decorated the house with pink balloons and streamers, trusting that Ana's intuition was correct.

Ana loved celebrating her baby: It was a new beginning, a chance to relive her childhood and to provide all the love and security to her baby that she wished she had had for herself. Ana was more optimistic about her future when she considered it through the eyes of her unborn niña.

Ana was so preoccupied with what was happening inside her body that she had little time to worry about leaving the hogar when the baby was born. In part, she didn't want to imagine life outside the hogar; she didn't want to think of being alone, living without Berto, or starting over in a new group home.

Silvia and Pablo spent hours on the phone, tracking down leads and trying to find the best place for Ana and her baby. Eventually, they contacted Ana's favorite aunt, Aída, who had been unable to take Ana several years before. This time it was different: Aída had a little more money from her job waiting tables at a restaurant, and her own children were a little bit older and more independent.

"A baby belongs with family," Aída told Silvia. "I would love to have Ana and the baby live with me."

When Silvia hung up the phone, she felt confident that Ana would be welcomed and supported as a new mother.

80

A month before Ana's due date, Berto was hospitalized; the pain in his hip had become unbearable, and he needed surgery to clean out the infection so he could regain use of his leg. Berto couldn't offer much support to Ana during this time; he needed to take care of his own health. He told Ana he was sorry he couldn't help more.

"It will be okay," Ana told him, but the words felt empty to both of them. For months she had imagined Berto standing by her side, holding her hand, stroking her hair as she delivered their baby; she knew there was nothing he could do about his situation, but she was very disappointed that the birth was not going to happen as she had hoped. Ana was afraid of the pain, afraid of possible complications, afraid of the unknown; she didn't want to be alone during the birth of the baby.

Ana tried to be strong for Berto. She visited him in the hospital a couple of times, but in the last few weeks, Ana's doctor told her to stay off her feet as much as possible because hers was considered a high-risk pregnancy. Ana quit school and rested at the hogar.

Ana couldn't get comfortable: She didn't sleep well at night; her big belly created too much pressure. She sometimes had nightmares, flashes of a beastlike figure that made her awaken in a panic.

On these nights, Ana often turned to the photo-copy of her mamá still pinned to the wall by her bed in the hogar.

She thought to herself: *Mamá, I'm scared. I'm scared to bring a baby into the world.*

She looked at her mother's young face. *You were my age when I was born. Were you scared, Mamá?*

Ana thought about her mamá often, and in these quiet moments in the night, she longed for her mamá in the same way that a baby yearns for the comfort of a mother's touch.

I wish you were here to help me, Ana thought. *I wish you could hold my hand. I want my baby to have a good life, a life without abuse or pain.*

Ana found comfort in thinking about her mother. She stared at the picture, just as she used to do when she was a little girl. When she started to feel safer, Ana closed her eyes and drifted off to sleep.

81

One night, Ana woke up with sharp cramping across her abdomen. She had experienced some tightness in the past few weeks as the muscles in her womb contracted and made her stomach feel as hard as an overly stuffed piñata.

The pain eased and Ana caught her breath again. She rolled over in bed, expecting to fall back to sleep. A few minutes later, the pain returned.

She knew this was it.

Silvia drove Ana to the public hospital.

"It's okay, Ana," Silvia said. "I will be waiting for you downstairs. You are ready for this."

"Can you call Berto?" Ana asked. She knew he couldn't be there with her, but she wanted to make sure he knew that his baby was about to be born. He was in the same hospital, on another floor, and he would be able to see her after the baby was born.

"And Silvia, gracias for everything," Ana said. "Berto and I discussed it, and we want you and Pablo to be the baby's godparents. We know that if anything ever happens to us, you would love and take care of our baby."

"Of course, Ana, of course," Silvia responded. "We would be honored."

82

Ana was prepared for surgery. The doctor had told her that she should give birth by cesarean section to reduce the risk that the baby would be infected with HIV. Ana was afraid, but she pushed the fear out of her mind; she would do whatever was best for her baby.

Ana lay on a gurney, and a man she had never seen before came up to her and introduced himself as her doctor.

"Where's *my* doctor?" Ana asked.

"She's not here," he said. "You'll be fine." This was not what she expected; she became more nervous.

Another man came in to administer anesthesia. He injected medicine into her spine to numb her from the waist down. He told her that she would be awake during the surgery but she would not feel pain.

A nurse hung a paper sheet across Ana's chest so

that she could not see what the doctor was doing. When the doctor began, Ana felt pressure and knew he was cutting into her belly. She thought of her father cutting up sea bass; the image amused Ana rather than frightening her. Ana closed her eyes.

Then she heard a wail, the sound of her baby's first cry. The baby's voice—her baby's voice—was so small and needy, yet fierce in its will.

"It's a girl," the doctor said. "A beautiful baby girl."

The nurse took the baby to be cleaned and checked. Ana watched as she weighed her baby and put drops in her eyes.

Tears slipped down the sides of Ana's face. She was overwhelmed with joy and optimism. She knew that her world would now be different, more difficult in many ways, but at the same time Ana felt that she was given a second chance at happiness, an opportunity to love and to be loved in a way that she hadn't been during her own childhood. Her baby was born, and Ana was reborn.

83

Ana named the baby Beatriz.

After the doctor finished the surgery, Ana was moved into the recovery room. A nurse wrapped Beatriz in a blanket—like a burrito—and brought her to Ana.

Ana held her baby against her chest and looked into her dark brown eyes. A nurse brought Ana a small bottle filled with formula.

"You will need to bottle-feed her," the nurse said.

"I remember," Ana said.

Ana had learned from her doctor and from training at her support group that HIV can sometimes spread from mother to child through breast milk. Ana also knew that chance was involved—about one out of three babies of HIV-positive mothers are born HIV-positive. Isabel had not been breast-fed, and she was not infected; she had been one of the lucky ones.

As Ana cradled Beatriz, she felt blessed. Ana watched, mesmerized by her baby's beauty, amazed that those perfect little fingers had come from her.

Ana knew that she would do anything to keep her baby healthy. The doctor had assured her that because she had taken her medication every day, the odds were high that Beatriz would not be infected with HIV.

Ana thought about her mother; she flashed back to the memory of her mamá standing behind the bathroom door weeping over Lucía's death. For the first time, Ana understood her mother's pain.

Ana looked at Beatriz—her dark eyes, her head topped with brown fuzz, and her delicate body—and she knew that her daughter would be the center of her life. Ana was overcome with a depth of love that she had never felt before, a perfect love between a mother and child, the same love she knew that her mother had felt for her.

84

The minute Berto heard that his niña had been born, he wanted to run down to meet her, but he didn't have the strength to walk across the room. The nurse told him to rest and visit Ana and the baby in the morning.

As soon as he woke up the following day, Berto limped downstairs, with a metal walker, to the maternity wing of the hospital. The walker made an annoying nails-on-the-chalkboard sound that embarrassed Berto. He felt ashamed of his dependence on the metal contraption, so he left it outside the door to Ana's hospital room before he went inside.

He paused outside Ana's door to catch his breath and wipe the beads of sweat from his brow. He inhaled a deep breath of air, then pushed open Ana's door.

Berto used the railing of the hospital bed to guide

195

himself closer to Ana. With considerable effort, he sat on the edge of the bed.

"Hola, mi amor," Berto said, gently nudging Ana awake.

"Hola, hey, have you seen her?" Ana asked, her voice raspy. "Did you meet our niña, our Beatriz?"

"No, I haven't," he said sullenly. "I wanted to come yesterday, but the doctors told me I need to wait until I'm better."

"Don't worry. There will be time," Ana responded. She knew Berto was embarrassed by his dependency.

"Ana, I'm proud of you," Berto said.

"I know, I know," she said, smiling.

Their conversation was interrupted by a knock on the door. A nurse entered and said, "Ana, someone is here to see you."

Isabel walked into the room holding a single pink balloon. Ana was surprised. Was this Isabel—her Isabel—standing in front of her? They wrote letters and occasionally spoke on the phone, but Ana had not seen her sister in more than a year.

Isabel rushed to Ana, tears in her eyes.

"Oh, Isabel, I am so glad to see you," Ana said, embracing her sister. "You can be the first to meet Beatriz."

Isabel wiped her tears and kissed Berto on both

cheeks. She had already heard a lot about him.

The nurse came back to the room. "Berto, you need to go back to your room. You should not see other visitors right now." Berto's immune system was so weak that he could not be exposed to anyone who might be sick.

Berto kissed Ana. "Nice meeting you, Isabel," he said. "I promise we'll all be together soon." He left quietly.

The nurse returned with Beatriz. Isabel whispered, "She is so beautiful, Ana."

"Do you want to hold her?" Ana asked.

"Oh, no. I'm scared. She's so tiny," Isabel said.

"You are her tía, Isabel," Ana reminded her sister. "You are one of the most important people in her life. Hold her, don't be nervous."

Isabel held her niece stiffly. Her face lightened when she looked at the baby. A moment later she handed Beatriz back to her mother.

Ana and Isabel talked while Beatriz took her bottle. Ana told her sister that she worried that Berto might not be able to get a job because of the damage to his hip. How could he work when he spent so much time in the hospital? Without Berto to help out, Ana worried that she would be unable to support her daughter. She told Isabel that the doctors thought the baby was healthy. She told her that she and the baby were going to go home to live with their aunt Aída.

"Will she let me live with her, too?" Isabel asked.

"Aren't you fine at your godfather's house?" Ana asked.

"Of course," Isabel said, but Ana sensed something in her sister's voice. "I just want us to be together— you and me and Beatriz. That's all."

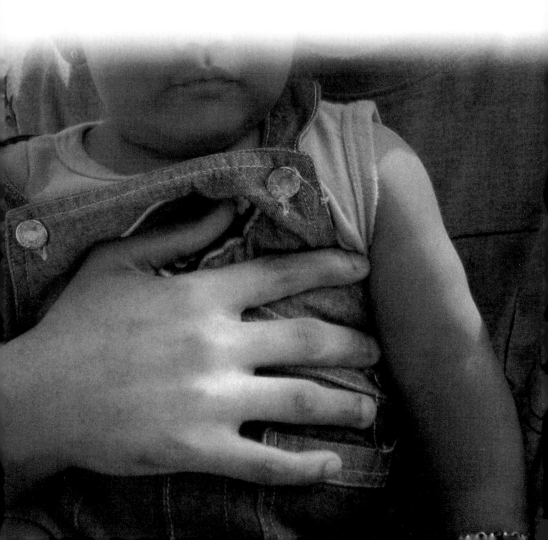

85

Two days later, Aída came to the hospital to take Ana and Beatriz home. Ana was exhausted but excited to see her aunt.

"Hola, Ana," Aída said, giving Ana an enthusiastic embrace. "Let me see the baby! Where is she?"

Aída picked up Beatriz from the bassinet. "She is so bonita, so pretty. She has her grandfather's eyes," she said, speaking about her oldest brother, Ana's own father.

"Thank you," Ana said proudly. Then she added, "Thank you for everything." Ana was pleased to be returning to her family, to what could be a permanent home.

"I only wish I could have done this years ago," Aída said.

Aída drove up to a small cinder-block house with

metal bars covering the windows. The house was in a poor barrio outside the city, where tiny houses painted bright tropical colors lined the streets. There were two small bedrooms, a kitchenette, and a living room for Aída, her husband, and her three children. Ana didn't care about the lack of privacy or the crowding. She was grateful to be with family.

Ana moved her box of clothes into the room she would share with her three young primos, her cousins. Ana hung her clothes on a pole mounted to the wall behind the bed she would share with Beatriz; the crib would not fit in the room. The room was littered with baby bottles, Barbies, remote-control cars, and piles of children's clothes. Ana was too tired to worry about the mess.

She placed Beatriz in the middle of the bed and used two pillows to create a barrier on one side; Ana lay down on Beatriz's other side and promptly fell asleep.

The next morning over coffee and fried corn patties with cheese, Aída and Ana talked.

"Do they know if the baby is healthy?" Aída asked, concerned about the possibility that the HIV could have been passed to Beatriz.

"The doctor thinks she's fine," Ana said. "But they'll need to do some tests later."

"That's a relief," Aída said. "I remember when you were so sick. Your abuela was so worried."

"When was I sick?" Ana asked as she sipped her coffee. "I've never been sick."

"Haven't you heard the story of how your abuela saved your life?"

While she knew that her abuela had taken care of her when she was young, Ana had never heard any stories about her abuela saving her life.

"When you were four, your abuela took you to the hospital, where the doctor said that AIDS was close to

killing you. You were thin—very sick and unhealthy looking," Aída told Ana.

"You lost all of your baby teeth, and you were near death," she continued. "Your abuela was determined to get the medication to save your life. She had to find a program in the United States to give you your medication when you were little. It was not an easy time for her."

Was Tía Aída talking about the same abuela—the one who beat her, the one who taught Ana to keep secrets? Ana had never heard this.

"I don't remember any of that," Ana said to Aída. Ana was happy to learn this piece of her past. Ana's abuela, her strong, proud, stubborn abuela, had loved her enough to fight for her life. This was important to Ana; it was important to know Abuela had loved her.

86

When Beatriz was six weeks old, Ana wanted to show her off by taking her to church in the hogar. That Sunday, it was raining heavily, but Ana decided to take the baby to visit.

After Mass, everyone surrounded Ana and Beatriz; the room was filled with the sweet hum of family. Ana sat proudly, cradling Beatriz, while her friends from the hogar gathered around her to admire the baby. Berto sat quietly in the chair next to Ana, but he didn't take part in the conversation.

Suddenly Beatriz broke out into a muffled whine. Ana rocked her and wiped the tears from her eyes. Berto handed Ana a clean cloth, but he didn't speak.

When it was time to leave, Ana held Beatriz with one arm and extended her other to Berto, who needed both Ana's arm and a cane to walk. She knew

Berto had been distant because of the pain he felt in his hip, but he was not acting like the Berto she had met under the tree at the reform center.

87

Ana spent most of her days without Berto. He lived in the hogar and was constantly in and out of the hospital. Aída and her husband worked during the days, and Ana's cousins attended school. Ana enjoyed the quiet and the time alone with Beatriz.

In the afternoons, Ana would put on a CD of one of her favorite bands, Aventura. She sang along, using the remote as her microphone. She often reached down and scooped up Beatriz, twirling around the small living room like a ballerina in a jewelry box with her daughter held close to her chest. Sometimes Ana danced to the bachata, her feet moving back and forth like a dial on a clock as she sang along to the words.

Ana's beauty was striking; her brown skin, long waves of dark hair, and dark almond eyes resembled the exotic subjects in Gauguin's Tahiti paintings. She was teaching her baby to dance the same way Papá had taught her.

88

When Beatriz was three months old, her doctor gave her an HIV test. Ana held her baby as the nurse drew the blood, offering a silent prayer that Beatriz would not be infected.

A few weeks later, she received a letter from the doctor's office. The results: negative.

Ana would not allow herself to relax completely; follow-up tests would be required in several months.

89

Berto returned to the hospital and stayed there for another month. He had missed the excitement of the holiday season—admiring the palm trees adorned with red and green lights, shopping for the perfect gift for Beatriz's first Navidad, taking his daughter to the annual Christmas parade. Ana had hoped to do these things with Berto, as a family; instead, she and Beatriz did them alone.

At the hospital, Ana rode the elevator to Berto's floor. The hallway had been decorated for Navidad with enormous red and green Christmas bells, which hung like monkeys from the ceiling. A Christmas tree with all its trimmings stood in the corner.

Ana walked into the stark, white shoe box of a room that Berto shared with his roommate, a painfully thin man who wore oversize diapers. Even though he was in his forties, he had been reduced to the humiliation of infancy. The man was half covered by a thin wool blanket, and his lifeless leg hung off the side of the bed. It reminded Ana of a hollow branch of a rotten tree.

Ana ignored the look of death in the roommate's eyes. She focused on Berto. He was dressed in a loose hospital gown. His face looked angular and skeletal; his skin was covered with a rash typical of those infected with AIDS. His thin lips rarely smiled anymore.

Ana brought Berto a box of shortbread cookies. She ripped into the plastic cover and opened the box. She bit into a cookie and then ran to the trash can and dramatically spit out the cookie. She wanted to cheer Berto up.

Even though Berto's eyes were still focused on the television, he quietly laughed. He was trying to play it cool.

Ana tried to force Berto to sample the cookie. The cat-and-mouse flirting continued until he pulled her close to him.

Berto was timid and introverted, but he was enamored with Ana. Pictures of Ana and Beatriz were taped throughout the room.

Ana sat on the edge of the bed and told Berto stories about Beatriz rolling over for the first time.

"I want to go home and see her do it," Berto said. Beatriz was not permitted to visit the hospital because she was so young.

"I want that, too," Ana said. Ana did want Berto to be involved in Beatriz's life, and she would have loved for them to be together as a family, but Ana had started to wonder whether Berto was the one for her.

Outside the hospital room, three nurses gossiped at the desk while sorting through death certificates.

90

Although Ana's barrio was a twenty-minute bus ride from Berto, she loved living at Aunt Aída's. She loved belonging to a family. Ana liked walking the streets of her neighborhood, passing mothers outside watching their children play and men cutting grass with machetes on the side of the road. Ana liked the fact that she and her Beatriz lived close to where she lived when she was a little girl and her mamá and papá were still alive.

Sometimes in the mornings, after Beatriz had been bathed and dressed for the day, Ana walked from her aunt's house to the supermarket a few blocks away to buy milk and diapers. One morning, two girls her age stopped Ana a block from her home.

"Hola, are you new around here?" said a petite girl.

"Sí," said Ana. "I moved into my tía's house about

three months ago. It's the peach one on the corner."

"I can't believe we haven't met. Is that your bebé?" asked another girl.

"Yes, this is Beatriz," said Ana, warming up a bit. "She is almost five months old."

"She is super linda, so beautiful and chubby," said the petite girl. "Hola, Beatriz, I'm Marcela and she is Verónica."

"I'm Ana. Mucho gusto," Ana said, thrilled to meet friends her age.

Verónica and Marcela walked with Ana and Beatriz to the park, where they met their amigas for a couple of hours every evening.

"You should come tonight. We have some cute guy friends. Do you have a boyfriend?" Verónica asked.

"Yeah, where is Beatriz's papá?" Marcela chimed in.

"Well, he lives nearby. Things have been kind of strange with him lately, though," Ana said, looking at Beatriz. She felt as if those words betrayed Berto, and yet she wanted to talk with someone about the strain in her relationship with him. But she didn't want to tell her new friends that Berto had been in and out of the hospital for months. She didn't want them asking questions about his illness—or hers. She just wanted some friends, she wanted to be thought of as a normal seventeen-year-old girl because that's the way she saw herself.

That evening at the park, Ana met their friends. She didn't remember most of their names, and she spent the evening next to Verónica and Marcela.

"Who is that?" Ana asked, pointing to a tall boy with broad shoulders and curly black hair.

"That is Guillermo. He is so guapo," Verónica said. "He lives with his mamá."

As soon as he looked in her direction, Ana shifted her eyes and turned toward Beatriz.

91

Things became more and more difficult between Ana and Berto. He had left the hospital and returned to the hogar, but they hadn't spent much time together. Ana always had to visit Berto because it was difficult for him to get around. She felt bad for him, sad he was in pain, but she also felt lonely watching other couples walk hand in hand with their children. Ana was surrounded by families, but although Berto was the father of her baby, she did not feel they were a family of their own.

Ana's feelings for Berto were unpredictable. When she thought of the love they shared in the beginning of their relationship, she wanted to be with him forever. When she thought of Beatriz, she wasn't sure that Berto could be the type of father that she wanted for her daughter. When they were together, Berto seemed more interested in Ana than Beatriz; it was as if Berto wanted to be a boyfriend, not a father. Ana wanted a family for her daughter. She wanted to give her everything she hadn't had.

In many ways Berto was still Ana's best friend, but she didn't have the same feelings for him that she used to. The passion, the attraction, the butterflies had flown away.

Instead, Ana found herself thinking of Guillermo. Berto was and would always be Beatriz's papá, but Ana knew what she had to do.

Ana didn't want to hurt Berto, but she had to tell him how she felt. Her palms sweating, she dialed the number of the hogar.

"Hola, Berto," Ana said nervously.

"Hola, Ana. What's up? How is Beatriz?" Berto asked, his voice weak.

"Beatriz is good; I'm good, too," Ana said as she cleared her throat. "Berto, there is something I need to talk with you about. I know I've been acting weird."

"Ana, it's fine," Berto said, trying to cut her off. "I understand."

"No, Berto, it's not okay." Ana paused, unsure of how to say it. Then she blurted out: "You will always be Beatriz's papá, but I don't think we are working as a couple."

There was silence on the phone line.

"I wasn't expecting this at all," Berto said. "I don't want this. I don't want Beatriz to live the life that I have lived, without a mamá and a papá. I am her father."

Ana couldn't respond. She knew his pain, and she didn't want to add to it.

"I would do anything to make this work, to be a family, a real one," he said.

"Berto, you can't. You don't have a job. You still live in the hogar. You need to be there, but Beatriz and I can't live there with you. How can we be a family when we can't live together?" Ana said. Then she realized that there was more to it.

"I'm sorry, but my feelings have changed, too," Ana said.

"Okay" was all Berto said; then he hung up the phone.

Ana felt a combination of grief and relief. She didn't regret what she had done, but she did regret that Berto would not be able to be the kind of father Beatriz needed. Ana and Berto still wanted the same future—one with a loving and supportive family—but Ana no longer saw them living that dream together.

92

On New Year's Eve, Verónica stopped by Ana's house.

"Hey, what are you going to do tonight?" Verónica asked.

"Nada," Ana said. "I think I'm going to stay home with Beatriz."

"No way! You have to come to the park tonight. The boys are grilling fish and plantains and shooting off fireworks," Verónica said.

"I don't know. I can't stay until midnight; it will be too late for the baby," Ana said.

Aída overheard the conversation from the other room. "Ana, I'll watch Beatriz," she said. "You should go."

"Are you sure, Tía? This would be my first night away from Beatriz."

"Yes, get out of the house. Have fun," her tía said. "Beatriz will be okay."

Ana's Story

Ana and Verónica went to the park at nine. It was already full of kids dancing, lying on blankets, staring at the sky, and eating ice cream and Sno-Kones. The romantic sound of reggae filled the breezy air. The night was black, and a sliver of the moon hung in the sky, lit with fireworks.

Guillermo walked up to Ana and Verónica.

"Hola, Guillermo. Happy New Year," Verónica said, hugging her friend. "This is Ana. She and her baby just moved here."

"Wow, Cupid has hit me with his arrow," Guillermo said, his voice like rough silk.

Ana couldn't help but notice how Guillermo made her heart jump slightly.

He looked directly into Ana's eyes. "Do you want to dance?" he asked, reaching out to take her hand.

93

The following morning, Ana took Beatriz back to the hogar to visit her papá. When she arrived, she saw Berto standing in the courtyard, leaning against a cane.

"Hola, Berto," Ana said as she politely kissed him on the cheek. "How are you?"

"I'm fine," he replied, but Ana could see the sadness on his face. Berto left and went alone to his room.

Ana talked to Silvia and some of the women from the hogar about the date of Beatriz's baptism. She then walked down to Berto's room.

She remembered the nights she lay on Berto's small cot and listened to his heart beat in time with the songs on the radio. She was sad that her feelings had changed, but they had.

"What's up?" he asked.

"I just wanted to let you kiss Beatriz before I left,"

Ana said, handing Beatriz to her papá. He held her close and kissed her on the forehead.

"I'll do what I can to support her, and I know the hogar wants to help," Berto said.

Ana was pleased that Berto wanted to take his responsibilities as a father seriously and do whatever he could.

"Thanks," she said, reaching for Beatriz. "See you later." As Ana turned to leave the room, she looked toward the bed and saw pictures of herself and Beatriz taped to the wall next to Berto's pillow.

She turned toward him.

"Are there days you want me to come by to let you visit with her?" Ana asked.

"Afternoons are best," he said. "I'm going back to school."

Ana was surprised but pleased. "Good for you."

94

Later that afternoon, Ana's extended family planned to get together at Aída's house for a party to celebrate the new year. Ana was nervous; she had not seen her abuela or her great-aunt Sonia in a few years.

Ana hoped that Beatriz could be a bridge to reunite the family; the first day of the new year seemed an appropriate time to start over. Ana was ready to make peace. While the painful memories had not faded, Ana knew she had made things difficult when she lived with her abuela and Aunt Sonia. Of course, Ana's behavior did not justify the abuse, but now she could see how she had provoked some of the conflicts. She was willing to try again, for her daughter's sake.

When her family arrived, Ana stood in the corner, cradling Beatriz. When Ana's abuela walked into the room, Ana was relieved that Ernesto was not with her.

Her abuela had aged; her eyes looked old and tired, and her face was as wrinkled as a prune, but she still wore her pride like a medal.

Her abuela locked eyes with Ana and walked straight toward her.

"Is this your baby, Ana?" she asked sharply.

"Yes, Abuela, her name is Beatriz."

"Look, my great-granddaughter," her abuela called out to the family. Then she hugged Ana and took baby Beatriz from her arms.

Abuela carried the baby to the other side of the room, showing her off to the rest of the family.

Ana did not need to address the past with her abuela. For now, talking about Beatriz was enough.

Later in the evening, Great-Aunt Sonia arrived. When she entered the house, Sonia looked around the room and then walked over to Ana. Her steps were slow and labored.

"Hola, Ana," her great-aunt said. "It is good to see you and your baby. I hope you have a nice new year."

"You too, Tía Sonia," Ana responded.

Ana pulled Beatriz in tight and took a deep breath. She had seen both of the women who had injured and rejected her, and she knew now that they no longer had the power to hurt her. In her memories, both her abuela and her great-aunt were big, powerful, and dominating. When she saw them this time, they both seemed shrunken shadows of what they had been. This time Ana felt that she could protect herself—and Beatriz if she had to.

Later, Ana sat on the edge of the couch, talking to her cousins. She looked around the room crowded with her family. She smelled sweet empanadas baking in the kitchen, and she watched the adults laugh and talk together.

She knew that her family was flawed, but she was surprised that she genuinely wanted to be with these people in this place in this moment. The only person Ana missed, and the one she wanted to see most of all, was her sister, Isabel.

95

At the party, Ana learned that Isabel had been kicked out of her godfather's house and sent to the reform center. Until that day, Ana knew nothing of the nights Isabel stayed out late or the way she rolled her eyes at her godfather when he tried to correct her; she had no idea that Isabel cursed at her godmother and some-times skipped school. This news made Ana ache. She knew that Isabel was crying out for help, and she desperately wanted to visit her sister.

96

Two days later, when Ana approached the reform center, it looked unchanged from the day she left. She saw the same mural painted in red, lime, and turquoise.

Ana waved at the guards who had worked there when she was a resident. She went into the administration office and proudly introduced Beatriz to her favorite guard.

"Ana, is this your bebé?" the guard asked.

"Yes. This is my Beatriz. Isn't she beautiful?" Ana asked.

"She is. She has your smile," the guard said while gently squeezing one of Beatriz's cheeks.

"She looks more like her papá," Ana replied, her heart sinking slightly.

"Do you know Isabel?" Ana asked, changing the subject. "She is my sister."

The guard looked surprised. "She's your sister? She's a troublemaker."

Ana cringed. She never thought of Isabel that way. She was always the quiet one who watched as Ana got into trouble.

Ana handed the guard a bag filled with a toothbrush, soap, face lotion, and a pink spiral notebook with a pencil. "Can I give her these?" Ana asked.

The guard looked into the bag and removed the notebook and pencil. "I have to confiscate these," she said, but her voice was kind. "The girls can't have paper or they write notes to the boys."

"I understand," Ana said, remembering how she used to scribble notes to José and Berto.

"Go to the cafeteria and wait," the guard said. "Isabel will meet you there in about five minutes; she is finishing her work in the garden."

Ana walked to the cafeteria and sat at one of the tables. She looked at the stage and smiled, remembering her fifteenth birthday.

Sitting in that room, Ana was struck by the parallels between Isabel's life and her own. Isabel would soon celebrate her fifteenth birthday locked inside the same detention center where Ana had celebrated her quinceañera.

After several minutes, Isabel walked into the room wearing the familiar T-shirt and shorts Ana wore during her stay.

Ana thought she and Isabel looked more alike than they ever had before, almost like twins. They both had deep-set mahogany eyes, full lips, and thick, dark curls. Just as twins connect during their time together in the womb, Ana knew that she and Isabel were linked by their past experiences, by their anguish and joy. Isabel was her sister, her family, and she would honor her promise to her father.

97

Isabel hugged Ana fiercely and kissed Beatriz on the head. She sat down and wiped the tears from her eyes. These were tears of frustration, loneliness, and fear. Ana had never seen Isabel look so desperate, so empty.

Ana listened as Isabel's problems flooded out of her like a river. Ana's heart ached as Isabel told her, "All I want is to live with you, to live with Beatriz. I want to be with you."

Isabel looked Ana squarely in the eye and said, "Rescue me, please."

Ana remembered her father's last words to her: *Take care of your sister.*

"Isabel," Ana said, "I can't do anything right now, but when I turn eighteen, I will see if you can come live with me."

"That's one more year," Isabel said, her voice weak.

"I understand you quit school," Ana said, changing the subject.

"I can't stand it. You're lucky; you don't have to go," Isabel said.

"I wish I could go," Ana said, anger rising in her voice. "I can't leave Beatriz. I can't give her to someone I don't know, someone who might hurt her." This was the first time Ana truly understood how much she feared for her daughter. She didn't want to leave her in a situation in which Beatriz could be hurt the way she had been.

"I want to finish school," Ana said. "Now I can't even afford the uniforms, not to mention the books."

For a moment, both of the girls felt their own pain, their own regrets.

"At least you have Beatriz," Isabel said finally. "You're not alone."

Ana knew how lost and alone Isabel felt. She had felt that way once, too.

"It's not easy having a baby," Ana said gently. "I don't regret for a moment bringing Beatriz into this world, but it's hard. I can't do anything without her. I'm exhausted from changing her diapers and taking care of her all the time."

Isabel started crying, and Ana passed Beatriz to her. Beatriz let out a small whine.

"Oh, Beatriz, don't cry," Ana said. "This is your aunt Isabel, and we both love her very, very much."

98

When she was six months old, the doctors gave Beatriz a second HIV/AIDS test. This test confirmed the results of the first, but Beatriz would need a final test to definitively prove that she did not have HIV.

99

Ana began to see Guillermo more often at the park in the evenings. Guillermo loved holding Beatriz and making faces at her. He carried the baby on his shoulders, holding her upright and showing her off to all his friends. Ana liked that Guillermo took such an interest in her daughter.

A week after the New Year's party, Guillermo stopped by Ana's house.

"Hola, guapa," he said. "I've missed seeing you at the park the last couple of nights."

"I know. Where have you been?" Ana asked, hoping she sounded casual.

"I got a job," Guillermo said. "I've been too tired after work to come to the park. Anyway, I stopped by to see if you and Beatriz would like to come over tonight and meet my mamá."

No boy had ever asked her to meet his parents

before. She was sure Berto would have introduced her, but he didn't have parents. She felt guilty for thinking this, but she pushed Berto from her mind and responded, "I would like that."

100

That night Guillermo showed up at five minutes past seven, dressed in a white shirt and jeans. Ana had tried on four different shirts before deciding on a flowing light blue skirt and white tank top. She had woven her hair into an intricate braid.

Ana and Guillermo walked hand in hand, with Beatriz balanced on his shoulders, his free hand holding her securely. He guided Ana along the dirt roads to his house, one similar to Aída's, except it was lime green.

When they walked inside, Ana found Guillermo's mamá sitting on a tattered red couch.

"Mamá, this is Ana and Beatriz," Guillermo said.

"Ana, I've wanted to meet you," his mother said. "What have you done to my son? He met you and now he has found a job. I think you and that niña of yours have something to do with it."

Ana could feel herself blushing. She had no idea how much Guillermo cared for her and her daughter. It made her very happy and hopeful.

101

Ana started to develop more serious feelings for Guillermo. They spent almost every evening together, and he bought diapers and milk for Beatriz.

The three of them sat night after night on an old wool blanket in the park, enjoying the windy evenings of spring. They talked about their lives; Ana opened up about the guilt she felt for breaking up with Berto and for leaving Isabel at the center. She told Guillermo the stories of her past, but when she told them this time, they felt like they had happened a lifetime ago.

Ana wanted to be open and honest with Guillermo about everything. She wanted, most of all, to trust him with the secret of her HIV infection, but she was afraid of his reaction, his rejection.

One night, as they lay together in the park, Guillermo began kissing her more intensely.

"Guillermo, stop," Ana said. "I want to take this *very* slowly." Ana refused to get intimate with Guillermo until she told him the truth.

Ana thought about Papá, who had been infected with HIV/AIDS by her mother. When her parents met, her mother was thirteen years old, and she was unaware of the disease inside her. Ana's mamá didn't know that her love would make Papá so sick.

Ana could not allow her infection to spread to anyone else. "My mother didn't know better, but I do," she said to herself.

102

Ana woke up in the night and stared at Beatriz. Her breath was slow and relaxed, like soft puffs of air.

"Mi niñita, te amo," Ana said quietly.

Ana couldn't get back to sleep. She felt anxious about Guillermo. She wanted to tell him she had HIV, but she was worried that he would leave her if he knew.

As Ana looked at Beatriz, she decided she needed to talk to Guillermo before their relationship went any further. Otherwise it would not be fair to him, or to her and Beatriz. If he couldn't deal with the truth and their relationship ended, Ana would have to accept that. If he embraced her as she was and wanted to move their relationship forward, then she knew it would be built on a foundation of truth.

Ana understood now that the truth was always better than secrets or lies. Before she had told anyone about her illness, Ana felt powerless and alone. Now she realized that it didn't have to be a secret; it was part of her, but it didn't have to control her. She was free to live her life as fully and responsibly as she could.

As she kissed Beatriz gently on the forehead, she was filled with hope for her future, a future no longer controlled by secrets but filled with openness, honesty, and trust.

The following night, Ana, Guillermo, and Beatriz spent the evening together. But this time, when Guillermo walked her back to her aunt's home, she asked him to stay and talk for a while. Ana stepped inside and put Beatriz to bed, then returned to the front porch, where Guillermo was waiting.

She took a deep breath and sat next to him on the step.

"Before we get closer," Ana told him, "there's something we need to talk about."

AFTERWORD

This book does not have a tidy ending, because it is a work of nonfiction based on a life in progress. Ana is a seventeen-year-old girl with a lifetime of choices ahead of her. When I last spoke to Ana:

- *She had told Guillermo she is HIV-positive. He has accepted her as she is, and they continue their relationship. If they decide to become intimate, Ana is dedicated to always using condoms. But even if their relationship goes no further, Ana's courage in being completely honest with him was a major step toward shaping her own life.*
- *Both Ana and Berto have returned to school. Beatriz is being watched by a trusted babysitter.*
- *Beatriz will have a final HIV screening at eighteen months to confirm that she has not been*

infected with the virus.

• Isabel has moved out of the reform center to an orphanage, where Ana reports that she is doing better. Ana still dreams of the day when she will honor her father's words and live in the same house with Isabel and Beatriz.

This book must end, but Ana's story is still being written—this time, by her.

JENNA BUSH

Dear Reader,

I hope you are inspired by Ana as much as I am. To me, her words and her life are like a song—a song of hope and resilience. I met with Ana for more than six months and listened to the melody and lyrics of her life, as we sat on her porch watching the day go by, or in her small living room, or in a café. This is her story—her song—not mine.

As the months passed, I was intrigued by Ana's complexity. She is only seventeen, but she is wise beyond her years. Once, when we discussed her first party and her first boyfriend, her eyes filled with the light and energy of a young girl. She giggled as she described walking from school to the party and dancing freely. Then Beatriz began to cry. She held and rocked her baby, and suddenly she wasn't a girl anymore . . . she was a caring mother.

One Sunday, in the meeting room of the church, she flirted with Berto like a teenager. Yet when they doted over their baby, she was a woman, loving and protecting her child. As she told me joyfully about swimming in the waves of the Pacific Ocean, she was a girl again. But as I walked out of the church and turned to watch her support Berto, who was now showing increased signs of AIDS-related frailty, she suddenly became an adult.

Ana is not alone in this dichotomy of children who grow up too soon. Many kids around the world are forced to take on the responsibilities of adults before they are ready. Often their childhood ends prematurely because they are orphans, live with illness, disability, or in extreme poverty. Some are forced to work at an early age instead of going to school. These children are excluded from living with the basic necessities. They do not have adequate food, clothing, shelter, or access to decent medical care and education.

With the assistance of UNICEF and other organizations that help children, there is hope for kids like Ana. She has broken the cycle of illness, silence, and abuse by educating herself. She is determined to survive both for herself and for her daughter.

You may be asking, "What does this have to do with me? How can I help? What could I possibly do to make a difference?"

There are so many ways that you can make a differ-ence in your family, school, community, and around the world. These don't need to be grand gestures that require travel or a lot of money. Simple signs of friendship and acceptance can often change the lives of those on the out-skirts of society. You can also volunteer for programs that help those in need. In the following pages, you will find some ways you can become more aware of the themes of the book: HIV/AIDS, abuse, exclusion, and exploitation. You will also find ways you can get involved in helping to solve these crises around the world and in your town. Every child deserves a chance for a better life—a safe and healthy life. You can make a difference. You have the power to help kids find strength and hope—just as Ana has.

And if you need help yourself, don't be ashamed and don't keep it a secret. Look at the resources provided here. Talk to someone you trust at home or in your school, reli-gious group, or community. Ana didn't have many choices in her situation, but as more and more people become aware of children in need of protection, more programs and safe havens have become available to them. So don't be afraid to ask for help. Don't keep silent, don't feel ashamed. Remember Ana. Live like Ana and take the steps you need to have a safe, optimistic life.

YOU CAN MAKE A DIFFERENCE

There are young people throughout the world who live in the same conditions and face the same hardships as Ana. Whether you want to help globally, right next door, or from your computer, you can fight HIV/AIDS, abuse, poverty, and exclusion. Talk to your parents or caregivers about what you'd like to do. You can improve kids' lives everywhere. *You* can make a difference.

If you have ... an hour

EDUCATE YOURSELF.

Learn more about HIV, abuse, and programs that interest you by researching online or visiting your school or local library.

"PASS ON THE GIFT."

Donate money to buy cows, sheep, rabbits, honey-bees, ducks, and other animals to help hungry communities throughout the world feed and educate themselves. Heifer.org tells you how you can donate and other ways you can volunteer for Heifer International programs if you want to do more.

SHARE INFORMATION.

Use the discussion questions at the back of this book and your research to talk about the tough issues you read about in *Ana's Story*. The more you discuss the facts, the faster stigmas will dissolve.

If you have . . . an hour a week

VOLUNTEER.

Stop by or call your city hall or municipal building and find out if there's a volunteer network from which you can learn more about local projects.

BECOME A MENTOR.

Go to a community center nearby to find out if it has a program for younger kids who need older role models and friends. Or become a Big Brother or Big Sister at www.bbbs.org.

TEACH A SKILL.

Use your talents and interests by coaching a sport, sharing your culture, reading a book aloud to someone, teaching music, or leading an arts and crafts project in your community.

TUTOR A STUDENT.

Contact your local board of education to find out if there is a volunteer tutor coordinator for your district. Or call a school directly and ask how you can help a child.

PROVIDE SUPPORT AND COUNSELING.

Volunteer for an HIV/AIDS or abuse hotline. You'll have to go through some training, but after that's over you'll probably have to commit to only a few hours each month.

If you have . . . a day

Observe World AIDS Day on December 1. Talk to a person in charge and organize an event at your school, place of worship, or community center. Find themes,

toolkits, posters, and other resources at:
- www.worldaidscampaign.info
- www.omhrc.gov/hivaidsobservances/world/

If you have . . . a month

ORGANIZE DONATION DRIVES.

Contact a local shelter, hospital, school, or place of worship about organizations in the area that accept donations for those in need. Then get permission to start collecting. You might consider these ideas:
- An October coat and blanket drive
- A November canned food drive to help feed families who otherwise would not be able to celebrate Thanksgiving
- A December gift drive for the holidays
- An any-time-of-year drive for the basics: toiletries, diapers, and simple health-care supplies

If you have . . . a summer

MAKE TRAVEL COUNT.

Talk to your parents or caregivers about giving back during your school breaks and take a trip that's fun *and* fulfilling. Find a community service opportunity in another part of the world. Here are some suggestions on where to start:

- Academic Treks (www.academictreks.com)
- Lifeworks (www.lifeworks-international.org)
- World School (www.worldschoolinc.org)
- Habitat for Humanity (www.habitat.org)
- See if your house of worship is organizing any trips to work in another part of the country or world.

If you have ... a year

SPONSOR A CLASS.

Help out in an elementary school classroom. Organize a group to visit the students, raise money for supplies, or donate books to the room.

JOIN KEY CLUB.

The world's largest student-led organization asks members to commit to fifty hours of community service. If your school doesn't have a Key Club, start one. To find out how, log on to www.keyclub.org.

WRITE TO A PEN PAL.

Ask your teacher about exchanging letters or emails with students in a class in another country. This is a great way to meet new people in new places and find out more about their cultures, their countries, and their needs. And you can make interesting new friends.

Make a difference with UNICEF ...

UNICEF, the United Nations Children's Fund, provides lifesaving nutrition, clean water, education, protection, and emergency response in 156 countries. For more than sixty years, UNICEF has been the world's leading international children's organization, saving more young lives than any other humanitarian organization. While millions of children die each year due to preventable causes such as measles, treatable diseases such as HIV/AIDS, and as a result of violence, UNICEF, with the support of partnering organizations, donors, and volunteers alike, has the global experience and reach to give children the best hope of survival. Whether you have a little or a lot of time, think about supporting UNICEF's efforts.

VOLUNTEER FOR UNICEF.

Register online at www.unicefusa.org/volunteer to access special volunteer resources, take online training sessions, communicate with other volunteers, and learn the latest information about UNICEF's programs and volunteer opportunities.

TRICK-OR-TREAT FOR UNICEF.

Visit www.unicefusa.org/trickortreat for free collection boxes and information, then dress up and invite some friends or a younger brother or sister to go out on Halloween and collect money.

LEARN MORE ABOUT
THE STATE OF THE WORLD'S CHILDREN REPORT.

Educate yourself about UNICEF's mission to save children's lives around the world by reading the report at www.unicef.org/sowc07, and encourage your teacher to use online lesson plans at www.TeachUNICEF.org.

BECOME ONE OF THE VOICES OF YOUTH.

You can speak out on all kinds of issues, from health to abuse to human rights. To find specific ideas, check out www.unicef.org/voy/takeaction.

GET YOUR FRIENDS INVOLVED.

You can create your own fundraising web page and introduce friends and family to UNICEF. Log on to www.unicefusa.org/friendsaskingfriends to find out how.

Get involved

BE A FRIEND.

You never know whose day you might change with a little kindness. Inclusion and friendship are the first steps toward developing trust, and trust can open many doors.

TAKE ACTION.

You really *can* make a difference. Start small, but start.

PROTECT YOURSELF, PROTECT OTHERS

Ana's Story addresses the ways unprotected sex and sexual abuse spread HIV and how other forms of abuse, poverty, exclusion, and the lack of education put children in danger.

When it comes to HIV/AIDS and other sexually transmitted infections (STIs), STIs don't care what color your skin is, how much money your family makes, what country you live in, or how old you are. They can infect anyone who gives them a chance.

However, there are ways you can reduce your risk of contracting a disease or infection. By ending or reporting an abusive relationship, making smart decisions about sex, or just speaking up and educating yourself and the people around you, you can help protect yourself and you can be an example to others.

No matter what you've done or haven't done, or what's been done to you in the past, it's never too late to get the facts and take steps to protect yourself and the people you love.

If you're hurting, in trouble, or want guidance, speak with someone you trust—your parents, a sibling, a school counselor, or a religious leader. If you can't do that—for whatever reason—there are other sources of support and information.

Protect yourself from HIV/AIDS and other STIs

GET THE FACTS.

There are a lot of myths and misinformation about sex out there. There are also a lot of great resources where you can get the truth—like a doctor or a professional organization. Knowing the facts can help you decide what's right for you.

MAKE YOUR OWN DECISIONS.

By getting the facts and educating yourself, you can be empowered to make the decisions that are right for you.

Don't let anyone pressure you into doing something that makes you uncomfortable. Whether you choose to wait until you're married or older to become sexually active, give yourself as much time as you need to make a well-thought-out and mature decision. When you're ready, make sure your partner respects your choices.

REDUCE YOUR RISK.

There's only one way to be 100 percent certain you won't get an STI—abstinence. There are a lot of ways to show you love or care about someone without having sex. If you decide abstinence is right for you, don't let anyone tell you otherwise. But if you decide that you're ready for a sexual relationship, the best way to protect yourself from HIV and other STIs is to be faithful to your partner and use a condom every time. No exceptions—ever.

GET TESTED.

If you have unprotected sex, if the condom fails, or if you've been raped or sexually abused in any way, don't wait to find out whether you're HIV-positive or have contracted any other STI. If any test comes back positive, you'll be able to begin treatment sooner. That could be crucial to living a long, healthy life. And if you become pregnant, you'll be able to get information about taking care of yourself and your baby.

Protect yourself from an attack, abuse, and rape

Sixteen- to nineteen-year-olds are three times more likely than all others to be the victims of rape, attempted rape, or attempted sexual assault.* Remember that it's *never* your fault if someone attacks you, but there are ways to protect yourself.

STAY ALERT AND READY.

You may love your iPod or MP3 player, but turn it down or take your headphones out when you're walking or jogging in a place you don't know well. Be aware of your surroundings and the people around you. Let your parents or guardians know where you will be and when you will return. If possible, keep your cell phone in hand—just in case you need to call for help fast.

STICK WITH FRIENDS.

You go to parties, movies, or the mall to mix and hang

*Source: Texas Association Against Sexual Assault—www.taasa.org/teens/default.php

out, but it's always a good idea to come *and leave* with a group of people you know. You should also plan to check in with one another regularly.

GET OUT OF FRIGHTENING OR UNCOMFORTABLE SITUATIONS.

No matter where you are, when "no" doesn't work, leave. Say whatever you need to say to get out of an uncomfortable situation: "My friends and I were going to meet up. They're probably looking for me," or "My parents will be home any minute." Or just *go*. Don't worry about anybody thinking you're not cool—choosing safety is the coolest and most important decision you can make.

Get help if you need it

If you have been raped or sexually assaulted, the Rape, Abuse & Incest National Network (RAINN) recommends that you take these steps:

- *Go to a safe place.* Ask a friend or adult to stay with you.
- *Don't shower, brush your teeth, use the toilet, or change your clothes.* These activities can erase evidence.

- *Call and report the attack to authorities. Call 9-1-1 to report to the police if you have been raped or sexually assaulted.* You can also call the National Sexual Assault Hotline at 1-800-656-HOPE to help you understand what to expect if you decide to report the crime.
- *Get medical attention quickly.* In addition to having your physical injuries treated, you can talk to a professional about the risk of STIs and pregnancy.
- *Have a doctor or nurse perform a "rape kit."* This exam collects evidence such as hair and fibers. Having a rape kit done does not mean you have to report the crime—that's your decision to make when you're ready. But the evidence will be there if you do choose to report the sexual assault or rape.
- *Talk to someone.* No matter how long ago the attack occurred, talking about it can help. You can find a counseling center near your home by visiting the following website: tools.rainn.org/bin/counseling-centers.

It's still abuse if . . .

Abuse isn't always sexual. If you're being hurt in any way, anywhere, don't keep silent. Whether it's a girl-friend, boyfriend, or older adult in your life, no one has the right to threaten, hurt, or overpower you either physically or emotionally. If you are being abused, here's what you can do:

CONFIDE IN SOMEONE YOU TRUST.

Talk to a parent or family member, a friend, a friend's parent, a teacher, a coach, a religious leader, or some-one else you can trust. You can also contact a local youth services agency. To find one near you:
- Visit www.childhelp.org/get_help/local-phone-numbers.
- Call the Child Abuse Hotline at 1-800-4-A-CHILD.

BULLYING IS ABUSE , TOO.

Like other forms of abuse, bullying continues—unless someone stops it. If you're being bullied in school, at sports practice, in the neighborhood, or on the internet,

Stop Bullying Now suggests the following ways you can help put a stop to it:

- Talk to your parents, teachers, or coaches.
- If you can, stay away from the bullies until the bullying stops.
- Ignore your bullies as much as you can. Don't respond to emails, but print them out and save them to show to an adult.
- Stay calm. Bullies want to upset you. Stick up for yourself if it feels safe, then walk away.
- Find out more at http://stopbullyingnow.hrsa.gov/index.asp

It's not just about you

Protecting yourself can also help protect those you love. Making the decisions about sex that are right for you, whether it's abstinence or practicing safe sex when you're ready, also protects your partners. While you need to protect yourself, you also have an obligation to protect others when it comes to sex. Don't be selfish or careless, and be honest with your sexual partner—relationships are a two-way street in every way.

Be a friend

Anyone who has been sexually assaulted—or is being abused in any way—needs friends. Sometimes it's hard to know what to do or say. RAINN and the Teen CASA have a few suggestions for helping a friend who is working through tough times.

LISTEN AND OFFER SUPPORT.

Don't judge, and don't feel you have to say something. Let your friend do the talking, and don't betray the trust.

GET HELP.

It's best if someone who has been raped is examined as soon as possible, whether they plan to report the crime or not. Call your local hospital to find out if it has a SANE (sexual assault nurse examiner) or SAFE (sexual assault forensic examiner).

If your friend decides to report the rape or abuse to the police or authorities, be there for them. You can go to the police station or make the call to 9-1-1.

GET INFORMATION.

Put together a list of counseling centers, hotlines, and websites that provide information and help with recovery. Let your friend contact them when he or she is ready, or offer to make a call or do more research for specific advice about how to help in this particular situation.

REPORT BULLYING.

Let a teacher, coach, or parent know that someone is being bullied. You shouldn't encourage mean behavior; get help from an adult and put a stop to bullying in your school.

WEBSITES AND HELP LINES

Maybe you're in crisis or just curious about health or how you can help. No matter what kind of information you're looking for, you can go to reliable sources to get advice and answers. Here are a few you might want to check out.

adolescentaids.org
Adolescent AIDS Program,
Children's Hospital at Montefiore

Montefiore Medical Center will answer all your questions about HIV/AIDS testing, including why it's important and what you can expect. There's even a clickable map so you can find a testing center in or near your community.

hivtest.org
Centers for Disease Control and Prevention

How do you know if you're HIV-positive? Get tested. You can learn about the different types of tests and type in your ZIP code to find a testing center near you. You'll also get the 4-1-1 on National HIV Testing Day.

acsa-caah.ca
Canadian Association for Adolescent Health

Whether you're looking for information on your mental, physical, sexual, or social health, if it's a part of your life, it's probably covered here. Alongside discussions of condoms and STIs, you'll get the scoop on sports, homework, and the teen social scene and how they affect your health.

childhelp.org
Childhelp

This resource is for young people who are being abused or know someone who is. With tips and articles, resources, a child abuse quiz, and the misconceptions and facts about what happens when someone reports an incident, you'll get important information to identify and prevent all kinds of abuse.

iliveup.com
Live Up: Love.Protect.Respect

Set to a calypso beat, this Caribbean media campaign hopes that youth action and activism will help stop the spread of HIV/AIDS in the region. The Play Safe area features games, quizzes, and animation, and Talk About It allows you to submit your own poems, artwork, videos, and personal story.

rainn.org
Rape, Abuse & Incest National Network

The most comprehensive online resource for information about sexual assault, RAINN's online library highlights statistics, types of sexual assault and their effects, prevention, and the laws that can help you.

stopbullyingnow.hrsa.gov
Stop Bullying Now!

You may be getting bullied, or maybe you're the bully. Either way, the bullying needs to stop. With animated podcasts and games, this site has a lot of information about why kids bully and what to do about it if you see it, feel it, or do it.

No computer?
Want to talk to someone now?

Whether you're in crisis, just want to talk, or have a question, getting help and advice is a phone call away. As scary as that call can be, it's important to get the information and help you need to stay safe and healthy.

1-888-988-TEEN
Break the Cycle

For twelve- to twenty-four-year-olds and the people who love them, this service provides legal advice, counsel, and referrals to teens and young adults who are wondering what to do about an abusive relationship.

1-800-4-A-CHILD
Child Abuse Hotline

Professionals answer calls twenty-four hours a day, offering counseling and resources and assisting youth who wish to report abuse. The hotline provides translations in 140 languages.

1-800-656-HOPE
National Sexual Assault Hotline

The Rape, Abuse & Incest National Network's free and confidential hotline operates 24/7. The hotline has answered more than one million calls from sexual assault victims as well as their families, partners, and friends.

WHAT'S THE REAL DEAL?

TEN MYTHS ABOUT HIV/AIDS

VIVIAN MERCEDES LÓPEZ
Regional Project Officer HIV/AIDS—UNICEF
Latin America and the Caribbean Regional Office

MARK CONNOLLY
Senior Adviser—UNICEF
Latin America and the Caribbean Regional Office

1. You can tell if someone has HIV.
Truth: You cannot tell if someone has HIV by looking at them. No symptoms develop immediately after the initial infection, so most people with HIV are unaware that they have become infected. But it is

often right after initial infection that the person is most *infectious* and can transmit HIV to someone else, even though they look and feel healthy.

2. There is no need to get an HIV test.
Truth: Knowing your HIV status is your right and your obligation to yourself and others. If you know your HIV status, you can get early care treatment if you are positive, and if you are negative, keep practicing safe behavior to stay negative. The majority of people with HIV do not know that they have the virus, and that perpetuates the spread of the infection. Knowledge is power and prevention.

3. AIDS isn't a problem in the United States.
Truth: It is estimated that more than one million people are living with HIV in the United States. AIDS was first identified in the United States in 1981. In the late 1990s the rate of AIDS diagnoses slowed down, but between 2001 and 2005 the estimated number of diagnoses has been increasing a little each year.

4. Only homosexuals are affected by AIDS.
Truth: HIV/AIDS is a disease that affects humans. Both sexes are vulnerable to HIV infection.

Worldwide, the most common form of infection is through unprotected heterosexual sex. In fact, globally, there are about 17.7 million women living with HIV, and 2.3 million children (under age fifteen). Adolescent girls are at increased risk of HIV infection through sex for many reasons, including biological susceptibility, having sex with older men, not recognizing their partners' risk behaviors, or because of their vulnerability to violence, abuse, or rape.

5. There's a cure for AIDS.

Truth: There is no cure for HIV/AIDS, but AIDS does not equal death. You can live a long time with HIV before developing AIDS, especially if you have access to ARVs (antiretroviral drugs). There has been a lot of progress in the development of these drugs, but ARVs are not a cure. Many people claim to have cures, but the sad fact is that the cure does not yet exist.

6. Condoms don't protect you from HIV.

Truth: If you are sexually active, then condoms are the *best* way to protect yourself from HIV infection. When used correctly and consistently, condoms can provide an effective barrier, blocking the pathway of HIV during sexual activities. If you are on "the pill,"

DepoProvera, or Norplant, you still need to use condoms to prevent getting HIV or other sexually transmitted infections. If you are having oral sex, you also need to use condoms. You can use male condoms and female condoms. Both need to be latex to have the maximum protection. Remember, HIV infection is preventable!

7. You can get HIV from kissing.
Truth: HIV does exist in saliva, but there is no evidence that the virus is spread through saliva and there are no confirmed cases of infection by kissing. You can't get HIV from hugging, having meals and drinks, or sharing a bathroom with someone who is living with HIV. The body fluids that have high concentrations of HIV are primarily blood, semen, vaginal fluids, and breast milk.

8. You can't get HIV from someone on ARVs.
Truth: ARVs can help keep down the viral load in an HIV-positive person, and this will help keep them much healthier, but these drugs won't keep someone living with HIV from infecting someone else with HIV.

9. Two HIV-positive people don't need to use a condom if they're having sex together.
Truth: Practicing safer sex is important for HIV-positive partners too. Reinfection can happen, and this could impair the impact of the ARV medicines if drug-resistant strains of HIV are passed on from one partner to another.

10. HIV-positive women can't have children.
Truth: Women living with HIV can have children, and can have children who are not HIV-positive, thanks to medicines and special treatment that can be implemented to prevent HIV infection passing from the mother to the child. Without any interventions, though, between 25 and 30 percent of mothers will pass the virus to their newborn because HIV can be transmitted to an infant during the mother's pregnancy, labor, or delivery and through breast-feeding.

DO YOU KNOW THE WHOLE STORY?

TEN MYTHS ABOUT ABUSE

CLARA SOMMARIN

Child Protection Specialist—UNICEF

The Americas and Caribbean Regional Office

1. Children are rarely abused sexually.

Truth: Unfortunately, child sexual abuse is more common than you think. It happens every day. Exact statistics are impossible to track because many cases are not reported.

2. If somebody abuses you, it's *your* fault.
Truth: It is *never* your fault if you are abused. The abuser is responsible for his/her own behavior. It doesn't matter what you wear, what you say, or what you do, no one has the right to abuse you verbally, physically, emotionally, or sexually.

3. Touching or fondling is not sexual abuse.
Truth: Sexual abuse is defined as the forcing of sexual acts by one person onto another. It may be in the form of fondling, touching, intercourse, or exposing sexual parts of the body.

4. Children are only sexually abused by strangers.
Truth: Statistics show that most sexual abuse is committed by someone the victim knows and trusts—a family member, family friend, or someone else close to the child.

5. Bullying is part of growing up. It's not abuse and can't hurt you.
Truth: Bullying is one of the most common forms of violence in our society. According to the National Education Association, an estimated 160,000 children miss school every day due to fear of attack or intimidation by other students. Bullying = abuse.

6. It is a parent's right to discipline a child however they want.

Truth: No one—not even your parents—has the right to abuse you in any way. If you face any abuse at home, talk to a trusted adult and get help!

7. Abuse only occurs in poor and dysfunctional families.

Truth: Abuse can happen in families of all ethnicities and socioeconomic and educational backgrounds. Money, education, and appearances don't necessarily protect anyone from abuse.

8. If you don't talk about the abuse, it will go away.

Truth: Not talking about the abuse won't make it go away. Memories may be temporarily blocked, but the effects will often surface later in life. Telling a trusted adult or a good friend will help you confront the situation, put a stop to the abuse, and begin the healing process.

9. You can always tell when a person has been abused.

Truth: Signs of sexual, emotional, or verbal abuse are less visible than those of physical abuse. Every individual has a unique reaction to abuse. Some withdraw, some become angry and aggressive, and many just want to forget about it so they pretend it never happened. That's why talking about it is so important.

10. Children who are abused will abuse others when they grow up.
Truth: Many children and young people who have been victims of abuse heal and go on to lead normal lives like everyone else. Abuse in childhood does not automatically lead to aggressive behavior. However, being abused is not an excuse for becoming an abuser.

DISCUSSION QUESTIONS FOR

Ana's Story

Now that you have read about ways that
you can make a difference, use these questions
to discuss the important themes in the book while
or after you read it. Bring them to literature
circles or book clubs and start a dialogue about
Ana's Story.

1. Ana's prized possession is the photocopy of her mother's photograph. Why is this so important to Ana? Do you have an item that you cherish? Why is it important to you?

2. In chapter five, Ana's barrio (neighborhood) and her country are described. How is Ana's community similar to yours? How is it different?

3. Her grandmother warns Ana not to tell anyone she has HIV. Do you feel this was for Ana's own good or for another reason? What might her grandmother's motives have been?

4. In chapter eight, Abuela tells Ana that boys and girls are sometimes asked to leave school because they are infected with HIV. In what ways do their teachers violate their rights? Have you ever witnessed discrimination, and how did it make you feel?

5. Those boys and girls are excluded from their right to an education. In what ways do you see exclusion in your school? How has exclusion affected you? How can you help those who are being excluded in your community?

6. Why do you think Ana is worried about telling anyone that she's HIV-positive? Which events in the book create the feeling of fear of disclosing her secret? If you were Ana, would you tell? Why or why not?

7. After Abuela and Ernesto fight, Ana plays a game she calls Orphan. Why do you think Ana does this? In what other ways does Ana use her imagination to cope?

8. How do you feel about Abuela's response when Ana tells her that Ernesto has inappropriately touched her and Isabel? Do you think she really didn't believe her? How do you think Abuela should have responded? Why?

9. Ana decides to keep the sexual abuse she suffered a secret. Why do you think she keeps it to herself? What are some other things she could have done?

10. At Papá's funeral, Ana was angry with God. How do you think Papá's death changed Ana?

11. Ana's decision to write about her abuse in the letter caused some unexpected results. Did it lead to a better outcome for Ana, or worse, and how?

12. Ana goes through a spiritual journey with God throughout her childhood. At what points in her life does her spirituality undergo changes?

13. Ana's teacher, Señor García, tries to help her move into Yolanda's house. What are the roles that other adults play in her life? Why is this important? Who in your life supports you? List the five people who give you the most support.

14. Pilar tells Ana she had no choice but to sell sex in order to survive. Before reading *Ana's Story*, had you heard or read about other children who are sexually exploited? Do you think there is enough help available for children like Pilar? How can they be better protected? What can you do?

15. How do you feel about Ana's decision to break up with Berto? Was she being fair to him? What do you think Berto's rights as Beatriz's dad might be?

16. Ana is shocked to find out that her grandmother saved her life when she was a toddler. What do you think caused the change in Ana's relationship with her grandmother at the beginning and then again at the end of the book?

17. Do you think Ana has forgiven her grandmother? Would you be able to forgive someone who treated you badly? What would it take? Is forgiveness important?

18. Ana says that she wants to respect her father's dying words and protect Isabel. Why do you think the sisters are so close? What struggles does Isabel have that Ana may not have had? What struggles does Ana have that Isabel does not?

19. Of all the places that Ana has lived, where do you think she felt most at home? Where do you feel the safest, and the happiest? How is this place different from Ana's safe place?

20. Ana is only seventeen years old, but she has endured many hardships. In what ways does Ana seem like a teenager? In what ways does she seem older and more mature than her age?

21. In chapter sixty-six, Ana learns about HIV/AIDS from a local organization. What role does education play in Ana's story, both in school and out of school? How does education play a role in her future?

22. How much did you know about HIV/AIDS

before you read *Ana's Story*? Did you discover anything you did not already know about it? Do you think there is enough education and awareness about HIV and other sexually transmitted infections?

23. How did this book affect you? How can you help kids like Ana? What else can you do to help children break free from the cycles of abuse, illness, poverty, and silence?